COMPREHENSION QUARTERLY

CQ⁴

ISSUE A: Determining Important Ideas and Themes

From

A to Z

From A to Z

THINK ABOUT: Determining Important Ideas and Themes

NONFICTION
The Code Talkers
Read about the only unbreakable code of modern times.

A4

NONFICTION
Touch the Art!
Discover how the Blind create and enjoy works of art.

A11

NONFICTION
Signs of Progress
Learn how the Deaf communicate.

A25

FICTION
Sign Online
Can differences get in the way of friendship?

A19

DETERMINING IMPORTANT IDEAS AND THEMES

It's a Secret!

Addie has a secret ambition. She wants to be a supersleuth and fight evil throughout the world. So, to prepare for her future job, Addie is learning all she can about spies and the coded messages they send. One of her purposes for reading a book she found at the library recently, *Dear Ellen Bee: A Civil War Scrapbook of Two Union Spies,* is to enjoy the adventures of spies Elizabeth Van Lew and Mary Elizabeth Bowser. Addie also pays close attention to the kind of people the two women were and what the fearless spies for the Union needed to know to do their job.

Addie's purposes for reading— to enjoy spy adventures and to find out what it takes to become a master spy—influence how she understands *Dear Ellen Bee: A Civil War Scrapbook of Two Union Spies.* By **determining the important ideas and themes** in her reading, Addie gains a deeper understanding of this book.

Think about some of the different kinds of reading you have done lately. What were some of your purposes for reading? How did your purposes influence the way you read and what you understood and remembered?

What might be your purpose for reading "The Code Talkers," which begins on the next page? Thinking about your purpose before you begin reading will help you pay more attention to what's important as you read.

dibeh-yazzie dzeh ah-

attack

retrea

N A H

ane

BY TAMIM ANSARY

THE CODE TALKERS

bi -s o -dih
ah-nah jeha

The year was 1945. World War II was still in its terrifying last months. Somewhere on a tiny island in the Pacific Ocean, Sergeant Don Parker crawled through the jungle. He and his eighteen men were sneaking up on a Japanese foxhole. They were close now, only 50 feet away. Suddenly—kapow! Shells started crashing all around them. But the bombs were coming from U.S. guns on the beach!

"They don't know we're here!" the sergeant gasped. "We'll have to tell them." And he pulled out the radio.

But his men hissed, "No, Sarge! If you send that message, the Japanese will hear it, too. They'll know we're here. They'll cut us to pieces."

"Don't worry," growled Sgt. Parker. "We've got a Code Talker." He beckoned to Thomas Begay. The young Navajo crawled over to the radio. The sounds he uttered were unlike anything the men had heard. But a moment later, the shelling stopped. The message had gotten through!

Scenes like this took place hundreds of times in World War II. American forces sent countless secret messages which the Japanese never understood. Why? Because the messages were in code.

If you've ever belonged to a club, you probably know what a code is. It's a way of altering a message to hide its real meaning. The person who gets the coded message uses a "key" to change it back. For example, these three messages say the same thing in different codes.

kcatta

rfa5ntxsterabocswkk

buubdl

The first message is written backward that's the key. Read from the last letter to the first and you'll see what it says. The second message has extra letters. To decode it, read only every third letter (starting with letter 3). Can you figure out the key to the third message?

Secret codes have long played a crucial part in war. The Spartans of ancient Greece invented a clever one over 2,500 years ago. They wrapped a belt around a stick and wrote the message on the belt. When the belt was unwrapped, it looked like a column of random letters. When it was wrapped around another stick of the same size, the message appeared again. You and your friends can make a code like this with a long strip of paper and a broomstick.

What is your purpose for reading about secret codes? How will this help you decide what's important?

The Spartan code was useful until it was broken. In fact, almost every code used in war *has* been broken. One famous exception is the code of the Navajo Code Talkers.

The Code Talkers worked for the United States during World War II. America was fighting Japan in the Far East. Early in the war, the Japanese captured a group of small Pacific islands. From bases on these islands, they attacked countries such as Burma and India.

Then slowly, the U.S. took the islands back. The battles were savage. U.S. troops landed on each beach in a hail of bullets. They smashed their way through jungles in scattered groups. As they moved, they had to keep in touch with other units. They had to report what they saw, receive orders, and warn their fellow soldiers of traps and dangers. All this communication was by radio.

Of course, the Japanese had radios too. They could tune in and hear exactly what the Americans were saying. That's why the Americans talked in code. But coding and decoding messages took time. In the heat of battle, mistakes were made. Also, the Japanese were very good at breaking codes.

And each time they broke one, a new code had to be invented.

In 1941, an engineer named Philip Johnston had an idea. Johnston was raised on a Navajo reservation. The language of these Native Americans is difficult for adults to learn. It uses song-like tones as well as alphabetic sounds. The same word spoken in different tones has different meanings. In 1941, fewer than 30 non-Navajos knew this language.

What do you think the author wants you to know about code talking?

Mr. Johnston thought a code based on the Navajo language could prove unbreakable. He worked with 30 Navajos to develop such a code. In 1942, they put on a show for two top officers, Col. Wethered Woodward and Gen. Clayton Vogel. The Navajos coded, sent, decoded, and delivered a complicated message in 20 seconds. Regular army experts took 30 minutes to do the same job.

The officers were impressed, so the Code Talkers were sent to the Pacific. Eventually, over 400 Navajos ended up serving as Code Talkers. Without them, Japan might well have won the war.

The Code Talkers didn't simply speak Navajo. They created a code that *used* Navajo. They started by listing some 400 words that might come up in military messages—words like *attack, retreat, bomb, plane,* and *submarine.* Next, they thought of a Navajo word to stand for each of these words. Often they chose words from nature. Instead of *spy plane,* for example, they said *ne-as-jah (owl).* In place of *submarine,* they said *besh-lo (iron fish).*

The Code Talkers could also spell out words that were not on the list. For each letter of the alphabet, they picked a word that started with that letter. For example, they chose *apple* to stand for *A, bear* for *B,* and so on. They might spell *leg* by saying *Lamb Elk Girl,* except they said it in Navajo: *dibeh-yazzie dzeh ah-tad.* Who could possibly tell that these sounds spelled *leg*?

Experts often unlock codes by looking for patterns. In English, for example, the letter *e* comes up more often than any other.

But the Code Talkers could keep such patterns out of their messages. They had not one but three words to use for each common letter. They could spell *leg* by saying the words *Lamb Elk Girl* and *peg* by saying *Pig Eye Gum.* So *leg* would sound like this: *dibeh-yazzie dzeh ah-tad. Peg* would sound like this: *bi-so-dih ah-nah jeha.* No wonder the Japanese never broke this code!

The Code Talkers' finest hour came at the battle of Iwo Jima. This island lay directly between U.S. forces and Japan itself. Here, Japanese troops vowed to fight to the death. The marines landed on a steep beach. They fought their way up bare rocky slopes. Some 22,000 Japanese troops fired at them from caves connected by tunnels. U.S.

What's the important thing to know about the code created by the Code Talkers?

submarine
besh-lo
iron-fish

A7

officers had to keep their forces working together even with bullets zipping all around them. They could never have done all this without Code Talkers.

Some Navajos stayed with the commanding officers on ships sailing near the island. Others hit the beaches with the marines. During the first 48 hours of battle, the Code Talkers sent and received over 800 messages without one error. One month later, the marines planted the U.S. flag on Mt. Suribachi, Iwo Jima's highest point. Code Talkers were there to send out the news. Code Talkers were there to receive the news, too, on ships such as the U.S.S. Cecil.

The men who fought at Iwo Jima owed their lives to those few Navajos. Most of them never knew it, however. The Code Talkers worked under a veil of secrecy. They were asked not to talk about their work, even after the war. When they came home, therefore, they got no parades. Most of them returned quietly to the Navajo reservation. Their work remained unrecognized until 1971. In that year, President Nixon praised the Code Talkers for their role in the war.

Today, Philip Johnston and the Navajo Code Talkers are remembered as heroes—and legends. After all, they invented the only unbreakable code of modern times. ◉

If you remember two important ideas about the Code Talkers, what would they be?

CAN YOU READ THIS?

Create a code of your own. Use what you already know about codes to help you. Write a coded message to your classmates and see if they can crack the code. If not, provide them with the key so that they can read your message.

IN TIMES OF DANGER

The Navajo Code was unbreakable and helped the United States win the war. Besides using a code, how else might you send a message in times of danger? Write a letter to a friend explaining your idea.

THANKS, CODE TALKERS!

Make an award for the WW II Navajo Code Talkers. Decide what the award should look like and what important information to include. You may want to use traditional Navajo designs to decorate the award.

Totem Pole Tales

How do people leave a record of what they have done if they have no written language? The Native Americans of the Pacific Northwest used totem poles. Totem poles told their stories through carved figures. Some people believe totem poles can be read like books. But that's not true. You can identify many animals on the poles. But to know the whole story, you would need to know the complete history of the family that owned the pole.

The top figure on a totem pole was usually a family crest. Most often this figure was an eagle, raven, thunderbird, bear, beaver, orca, or frog. The figures were not always realistic, but you could identify them. The figures below the crest told a myth or legend or described an event from the life of a real person. Sometimes jokes were carved into the poles in the form of upside-down animals or little figures that peeked out of a bear's ear or a whale's blowhole.

Totem poles were carved from cedar trees. Frequently a chief carver and several apprentice carvers were hired to craft the pole. The chief carver carved the bottom 10 feet of the pole because that was the part of the pole that was at people's eye level. Even though cedar didn't usually decay, most totems fell over before they were 100 years old! Today, duplicates of the original totems are made by family members who own the poles.

Which animals can you identify on these totem poles?

Touch the Art!

*T*hese students are blind. They love the visual arts and know a lot about paintings and sculptures. They are taking art classes, have read books about art history, and have visited art museums. Some people might think that it would be impossible for a person who is blind to learn about art or to make art. Yet, there are many art programs and art exhibits for people who are legally blind or visually impaired. A person who is legally blind has only one-tenth or less of the vision that is considered normal. Being visually impaired means having difficulty seeing. Many different kinds of educational programs help the Blind learn about art and encourage them to create art.

by Eduardo Aparicio

Learning by Touching and Listening

The usual ways of teaching art, by looking at paintings or watching a slide show, do not work for blind students. New methods for teaching art to the Blind combine touchable materials with recorded descriptions and music. Blind students learn about art through a combination of touch and sound.

Using the sense of touch is a way of teaching the Blind. For example, the Braille alphabet, named after its French inventor Louis Braille, uses the sense of touch for reading and writing. Braille uses raised dots in different combinations. The dots represent numbers and the letters of the alphabet. A blind person, with proper training, can read Braille by touching the raised dots with the tips of the fingers.

Just as the Braille alphabet was made to be read by the Blind, works of art can also be adapted for the Blind. Paintings are being designed to be touched. These designs have raised lines, points, and patterns that show the lines and patterns of the original art.

A raised design of the original painting gives a blind person an idea of what the original work of art looks like, but it's not enough. Audiotapes that describe the painting fill in many details.

Recorded descriptions of a painting can include sounds that you might hear if you could visit the scene. For example, a recording for a painting of a beautiful meadow may include the chirping of birds and the rustle of the leaves in the wind. A recording for a painting of children at play may add the thumping of their feet

What do you think the author wants you to know about teaching art to the Blind?

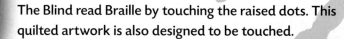

The Blind read Braille by touching the raised dots. This quilted artwork is also designed to be touched.

or their giggles. A picture of a neighborhood can be better understood with the recorded sounds of the street scene. These sounds help a blind person get a feeling for the place or the people pictured. Background music and sounds can also suggest a mood or a specific time in history.

Art Exhibits for the Blind

Larry Volk is an artist who makes artwork for the Blind. He creates big, touchable versions of the works by famous artists, such as Matisse, Picasso, and Warhol. He was inspired to do this by his blind grandfather. Mr. Volk includes Braille and raised white lines in his paintings. The method he uses produces images that can be seen by people who are almost blind. The images can also be touched by people who cannot see at all. The Blind use their fingers to trace Volk's pieces.

Many museums have special exhibits for making art available to people who are blind. Some museums have displays where the Blind can touch the sculptures. These displays often include wall labels in Braille and large print labels.

The Museum of American Folk Art in New York City has been very involved in making art available to the Blind. Several years ago, Irma Shore, who is legally blind, was a student at the museum. She discovered how hard it was for blind people to enjoy art museums. She made a list of museums

At this folk art museum, blind visitors are encouraged to touch the works of art.

that had exhibits for the Blind and created a directory. She also helped art museums learn how to set up art exhibits that were more interesting to the Blind.

Recently, The Art Institute of Chicago opened a new exhibition space called Touch Gallery. This is a permanent display of touchable art open to all. By being allowed to touch these pieces, blind visitors can discover facial expressions, hair styles, and other things about the sculptures.

The Touch Gallery includes five sculptures with text panels and labels in large type and

Are some parts of the text more important to the theme than others? Which parts? Why?

What do you think is the most important thing to know about the Touch Gallery?

Braille. The sculptures are made of bronze, marble, and stone. They all represent the human face, and they come from different time periods and places. One sculpture is from France, and it is a hundred years old. Another sculpture is from China, and it is over a thousand years old!

The interest of blind people in the visual arts is a benefit for everyone. Touchable art displays originally created for the Blind are now often available to all visitors. They are not reserved for blind visitors alone.

Touchable art exhibits make the experience richer and more enjoyable for all visitors. They allow visitors to feel and understand the artwork in new ways.

Art by Blind Artists

Tina Blatter, a blind artist who currently lives in Kansas City, Missouri, is well known nationally for her collages. In her artworks, she uses paint and everyday materials. She chooses different materials and layers them to express an idea or a feeling when seen or

Bronze sculptures like *Joan of Arc* and others from the Touch Gallery in Chicago allow blind visitors to discover facial expressions, hair styles, and other things.

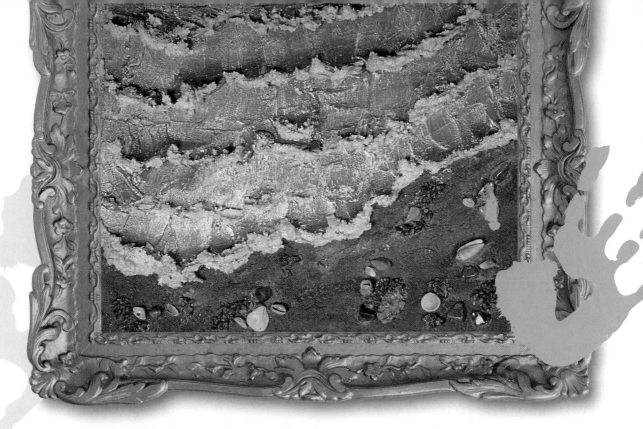

This artwork by Tina Blatter is titled *Beach Scene.* She carefully makes her touchable art so that it lasts a long time.

touched. The materials she uses are of different textures and weights. In some of her collages, Ms. Blatter uses tree branches pasted over canvas. She also layers foil and tissue paper in different colors, rice paper, clay, construction paper, ribbons, beads, and pieces of plastic foam painted to look like rocks.

In a series of collages about the ocean, she uses thick, plastic paste to shape the waves, Spanish moss, real sand, seashells, and polished stones. These materials create the illusion of water and waves.

When asked about her collages, Ms. Blatter explained, "By using various textured materials, I have been able to create collage art that is pleasing when seen or touched. People who are blind can enjoy them as well as people who are sighted. You just need to think what materials to use to make your idea happen. We all have our own feelings about expression, and it's up to you to discover what to use. The possibilities of expression are really limitless."

After reading the article, what are the most important themes and ideas to remember?

Stop and Respond

It's in the Bag

Ask a friend to put a small object in a paper bag. Don't look in the bag! Just reach in and close your fingers around the object. Write a few sentences that describe how the object feels—smooth or rough, heavy or light, curved or straight, soft or hard, and so on. Then remove the object from the bag. Look at the object and compare your written description with what you see.

Picture This!

Choose a painting or drawing you really like and think about how to describe it to a blind person. Use what you've learned about art for the Blind as well as what you know and feel about the work of art to determine what to include in your description. Then list some descriptive words or phrases that come to your mind. Finally, use the words and phrases in a paragraph or poem about the work of art.

Your Name in Braille

Locate the Braille alphabet in a book or on the Internet. Your purpose for reading is to find out how to write your name in Braille. Write your first name on a piece of paper and above each letter make the corresponding Braille letter. You won't need to make raised dots, just make dots with a pencil or marker. You may want to make a Braille nameplate for your desk.

DOTS and DASHES

In 1832, Samuel Morse thought of the idea for the electric telegraph while crossing the Atlantic Ocean on a ship. He is known as "the father of the telegraph." Years ago, the telegraph was described as an "instantaneous highway of thought."

Morse invented a code that uses a system of dots and dashes to represent each letter of the alphabet, the numbers zero through nine, and other symbols and punctuation marks. When you use Morse code, you have to spell each word in your message. (By the way, there's no spell-check on a telegraph machine!)

As a result of the *Titanic* disaster in 1912, the International Maritime Organization adopted SOS as the international distress (help) call. SOS does not mean Save Our Ship, Sink Out of Sight, or anything else, for that matter. It was just decided that ... --- ... (dot, dot, dot, dash, dash, dash, dot, dot, dot) was easy to remember.

Did you know that Thomas Edison used Morse code to propose to his second wife? Edison and Mina Miller used Morse code to have secret conversations when her family was around. They tapped the code into each other's hands. One day Edison asked,

.-- --- ..- .-.. -.. -.-- --- ..- -.- .-. .-. -.-- -- .

She answered -.-- . ... Use the Morse code key to read what they said.

Telegraph operators developed a shorthand for commonly used phrases and words. The end of a message was coded "30" meaning "I have no more to send." The code "73" meant "best wishes." "CQ" was a general call meaning "Hey, everyone, listen up!" And as early as the 1840s, "OK" was listed in telegraphy manuals to mean "That is correct."

A .-	M --	1 .----
B -...	N -.	2 ..---
C -.-.	O ---	3 ...--
D -..	P .--.	4 ....-
E .	Q --.-	5 .....
F ..-.	R .-.	6 -....
G --.	S ...	7 --...
H	T -	8 ---..
I ..	U ..-	9 ----.
J .---	V ...-	0 -----
K -.-	W .--	
L .-..	X -..-	
	Y -.--	
	Z --..	

DETERMINING IMPORTANT IDEAS AND THEMES

Elizabeth Van Lew: Patriot

Addie thinks *Dear Ellen Bee: A Civil War Scrapbook of Two Union Spies* is a wonderful, well-written, exciting book. The lives of Elizabeth Van Lew and Mary Elizabeth Bowser and their shared goal—to see slavery abolished and the Union preserved—fascinate Addie, a would-be spy herself.

As Addie reads, she finds herself thinking about the bravery of the women who could have been found out by Confederate soldiers at any time. Addie remembers an experience she'd had earlier in the year. She had tried to pass a secret message to a friend, and it had been intercepted by Mr. Porto, her teacher. How Addie's heart had pounded! How her stomach had flip-flopped! This personal experience helped her understand in a small way how Elizabeth Van Lew must have felt when she passed on coded messages about Confederate troops to Union generals.

By drawing on this experience and other personal experiences as she reads, Addie connects with the adventures of women who lived more than a century ago. Addie pictures their lives vividly, and the words she reads hold extra meaning for her. Addie's past experiences help her in **determining important ideas and themes** in her readings.

Think about a book you read recently. Which of your ideas and experiences helped you understand what you read?

TOP SECRET! FOR YOUR ONLY!

Sign Online

by Judith Zorfass

"If we don't hit a traffic jam, we'll be there in 15 minutes," said Grandma Anna before starting the car.

Fifteen minutes and then the waiting will be over, Greg thought as he buckled himself into the passenger's seat. The car ride was just long enough for Greg to review the events of the past months leading up to this very moment. It began last September when his Aunt Joyce, a teacher in Boston, e-mailed him a message describing her new class of 4th graders.

But after her "Love, Aunt Joyce," she had added a P.S. "Is it all right with you if I give Jon your e-mail address? The two of you have so much in common. You're both star hitters on your Little League teams, smart as whips, and mystified by your teenage sisters."

"I guess so," Greg answered. "If he writes first, then I might write back."

Jon wasted no time in sending the first, introductory e-mail. "I live in a town called Natick, just outside of Boston, MA. That's where Doug Flutie, the famous NFL quarterback, played football when he was in high school."

Two days later, Greg replied, "I also live near a big city, in a town called Skokie, just outside of Chicago, IL. Did you ever meet Doug Flutie?"

That first exchange started a flurry of messages between the East Coast and the Midwest. With each new message, the boys learned something else they had in common.

What do you think the author wants to tell you?

"I went ice skating for the first time," wrote Greg in November.

"I learned to skate when I was five by pushing a chair on a frozen pond near my house. I'm going to my friend's skating party next week," Jon wrote in December.

"My grandmother just moved to Tucson, AZ," Greg wrote in January.

"I can't believe it! That's where my grandma moved last year," Jon answered right back.

Their only disagreements revolved around baseball teams. "The White Sox are the best. I bet they make it all the way to the World Series," wrote Greg at the start of spring training.

"Good, maybe, but not as good as the mighty Red Sox," answered Jon. "I just know it will be their year."

But the biggest surprise came with the discovery that both boys planned to visit their grandmothers in Tucson for the same week during spring break. Jon suggested they get together.

"I really want to meet you in person."

Closing his eyes in the car, Greg remembered his confusion. His first reaction was an immediate *yesssssss!* He pictured them playing catch. But quick as a wink, his *yes* changed to *no, no, never!* For three days, Greg's computer screen remained black. If I don't even turn it on, I won't have to answer him, Greg reasoned. He trudged through each day feeling like a storm cloud shadowed his every move. Even hitting a home run with a player on third left him feeling hollow.

What do you think are the most important things to know about Jon and Greg?

At dinner one night, his mom noticed that he had hardly touched his favorite dinner, hamburgers and fries. "Greg, what's bothering you? You seem so gloomy. Are you feeling OK?"

"Nothing, it's nothing," Greg waved away her questions.

But when Dad insisted on knowing, Greg finally explained, "Jon and I have a lot in common. But I just never got around to telling him about the one thing we *don't* have in common—that I'm deaf. If we meet, he'll know as soon as I start signing. What if he doesn't want to be my friend anymore when he finds out?"

"We know it's hard to meet hearing people for the first time," Dad sympathized. "There's a moment of uncertainty. Will they accept me for who I am?" Dad's hands paused in midair as Greg nodded. Resuming, Dad offered his encouragement, "Somehow, from everything you've already told me about Jon, I don't think you'll have anything to worry about."

"Dad's right," added Mom, her hands in motion. "You already have what it takes to be good friends— lots of shared interests. The difference in how you communicate face-to-face isn't going to matter. Grandma Anna will be happy to interpret for you. She's interpreted for us dozens of times when we've socialized with our hearing friends."

> What ideas and experiences help you understand what you're reading?

Later, when he had finally logged onto the computer, Greg could still picture Mom's smile and feel her reassuring pat on his shoulder. Desperately wanting to trust that Jon would turn out to be a good guy, Greg typed,

"Sure, let's meet."

The American Sign Language Fingerspelling Alphabet

a b c d e f g

h i j k l m n

o p q r s t u

v w x y z

Happy

Meet

You

Online, their parents had made arrangements for the boys and their grandmothers to meet at the main entrance to the Sonora Desert Museum. Now, as they pulled into the parking lot, Greg felt his chest tightening. It felt just like when he stepped up to home plate with two outs. He might strike out; he might hit a home run. Who knew?

As the car came to a halt, Greg spotted a boy approaching them, waving both arms. Stepping out of the car, Greg's hands felt like lead. But knowing he had to return the greeting, Greg forced himself to sign, "Hi, Jon. You look just like your picture." Grandma Anna interpreted, giving voice to Greg's signs.

Greg watched Jon's eyes fix on his signing hands. Swallowing hard, Greg imagined all his worst fears about being rejected were coming true. How he hated it when strangers stared at him and his family in stores and restaurants when they signed.

Greg squinted, attempting to block out the sight of Jon's reaction. But even so, he still managed to catch a hazy glimpse of something so startling that his eyes shot wide-open. Jon's hands were moving. His hands were actually forming words—signs—that Greg recognized:

"Happy" (Jon's right hand, held flat, made a circular motion against his chest.)

"Meet" (Jon's index fingers extended upright, and his two hands came together.)

"You" (Jon's index finger pointed to Greg's chest.)

An incredible thought raced across Greg's mind. "Are you deaf, too?" The question flew off his hands as Grandma Anna voiced it.

Are there some parts of the story that are more important to the theme? Which parts? Why?

After shaking his head no and signaling to Grandma Anna to interpret, Jon explained, "Your aunt told me you're deaf and that you sign. I was waiting for you to tell me online but you never did. So I decided to surprise you. I'm learning from a girl in my class who's deaf. Her name is Jenny."

With furrowed brow, Greg shook his head back and forth slowly. "You knew all along? You never mentioned anything?"

With Grandma Anna filling in the missing signs, Jon answered, "Sure. But we had so many other things to write about. So now we both know." Finishing off the sentence with two outstretched palms face up and a shrug, he added, "So what?"

The boys planned another get-together later that week. But before they parted, Jon asked Greg, "Will you teach me more signs?"

"I'll start now," signed Greg. He then reached over and guided Jon's hands to form the word for *friend*, showing how the index fingers interlocked first one way and then the other.

"Looks like I'll be out of a job," Grandma Anna signed and said with a laugh.

"Sorry, Grandma Anna," Greg signed. "Pretty soon it will be a kids-only conversation. Who knows? Maybe one day, instead of writing to each other online, we'll find a way to sign online."

Jon smiled and shook his fist up and down in agreement, making the sign for *yes*. ●

What do you think the author thought was most important in the story? Why?

Friend

Stop and Respond

It's Personal

Think of a time when you met someone for the very first time. How does this experience help you better understand "Sign Online"? Write a paragraph explaining your experience.

Fitting In

Greg's biggest fear in "Sign Online" was that his e-mail buddy wouldn't accept Greg's most obvious difference—his deafness. Why do people worry about fitting in? Why do some people have trouble accepting differences? Write a short paragraph that responds to these questions.

Find the Signs

Jon is learning to sign. Look in the story and find the words that Jon has learned. Make a two-column chart with the word and the explanation of how to sign it. Add any additional words that you know how to sign. Practice signing these words with a partner.

SIGNS OF PROGRESS

by Jacqueline D. Greene

When you watch a baseball game, do you ever notice how the catcher and the pitcher send each other signals? The batter leans across the plate, ready to hit the ball. Behind him, the catcher squats low to the ground and drops one hand between his knees. As quick as a flash, the catcher's fingers move, sending signals to the pitcher. The pitcher then throws a curve ball, and the batter strikes out.

How does the pitcher know what kind of ball to throw? He simply interprets the hand signals the catcher uses. The signs let the pitcher and catcher communicate without talking.

Deaf people also can communicate with each other using signs. In the United States, the Deaf usually learn American Sign Language, which is also called by its abbreviation, ASL. It has its own grammar and way of putting sentences together. It is slightly different than the way you speak English. Most teachers of the Deaf believe ASL should be deaf children's first language. Then as these children grow older, they can learn English as a second language.

> What experiences have you had that help you understand what is important about communication?

Sometimes hearing people wonder why the Deaf don't just read lips. Reading lips is nearly impossible for any person who was born deaf. Even those who do learn lipreading can only recognize about half of someone's spoken words. If the speaker is not standing close by, the Deaf cannot see the speaker's lips clearly. This would be as difficult as reading a 2 inch sign on a stage while you're sitting in the balcony!

Nicole's goal is to become a sign language interpreter.

Meet Nicole Crossman

Nicole Crossman, a teacher of the Deaf, is studying at Northeastern University in Boston, MA, to become a sign language interpreter. Her goal is to become a certified interpreter.

Nicole studies at the university library.

Many years ago, Nicole recounts, the Deaf needed to have a hearing friend or family member help them communicate with people who did not understand ASL. The friend would interpret the signs from ASL into spoken English, and then reverse the process.

Nicole explains that there were some problems with this method of using family members or friends. Although these people wanted to help, they sometimes interfered in the deaf person's life. At times they changed what the deaf people were saying to what the interpreters thought they should say. Other times, the interpreter told a deaf person what to do or made decisions for him or her. This took away their independence, and often deaf people lost confidence in themselves. Just because they weren't able to hear didn't mean they weren't able to make their own decisions! Nicole describes how, in 1964, a group of individuals who worked with the Deaf decided to take action and make some improvements. A program was created to train professional sign language interpreters. No longer would

What do you think the author thought was most important so far in the article? Why?

the Deaf have to rely on friends or family members. Instead, certified interpreters who were fluent in both ASL and English would help the hearing and the Deaf communicate with each other, without interfering in the lives of the Deaf.

At Northeastern University, along with learning ASL, Nicole takes classes that explain deafness and teach about the different ways the Deaf interact with each other. For example, Nicole points out that when a hearing person approaches two people who are talking, this person usually does not interrupt them. However, Nicole emphasizes, the Deaf can't stand by quietly because they might not be noticed. When the Deaf see two friends signing to each other, and they want to join in the conversation, they tap one person on the shoulder and just begin to sign.

Another situation Nicole describes is when the Deaf must walk in front of another person. They can't sign *Excuse me* very easily, so the Deaf just step in front of the other person. Nicole points out that to the Deaf this isn't considered bad manners but is considered to be polite Deaf manners!

Nicole, like all people training to become sign language interpreters, must learn a special code of ethics. The code has rules about how interpreters should work with the Deaf.

After Nicole completes her courses at Northeastern University, she must pass a national exam. After passing this exam, she will earn a certificate proving she is a professional sign language interpreter.

Lindsay understands the value of a sign language interpreter.

Meet Lindsay

Lindsay is a deaf high school student who often has used an interpreter to help her communicate with hearing friends. In elementary school, Lindsay attended a public school in her hometown. She was mainstreamed in a class with hearing students. In order to understand the teacher's instructions and communicate with her classmates, Lindsay acknowledges, "It became a habit to have an interpreter every day." In classes, Lindsay also would have someone take notes for her so she could read what the teacher explained out loud.

Lindsay points out that some deaf people sign in English and that signing in English is very different than signing in ASL. The worst experience Lindsay had with an interpreter was when she was in middle school. She was assigned a sign language interpreter who signed in English. Lindsay admits that signing in English was like a foreign language to her because her first language is ASL.

Lindsay cites an example of how a sentence would be used in English and in ASL.

In English, a speaker would say *The train left.* But in ASL, the signer would sign *The train became smaller.* The sign used to show the train getting smaller is understood by someone who knows ASL to mean "it left."

Lindsay emphasizes the importance of a good interpreter also being able to understand a deaf person's feelings. When hearing people talk, the sound of their voice can help the listener understand the meaning of what is being said. The hearing person might laugh or use an angry tone of voice while speaking. Lindsay describes how sign language interpreters are able to convey feelings and moods, too. Interpreters do this by using facial expressions, body language, and eye movements. As Lindsay puts it, interpreters using ASL behave like actors on a stage.

What do you think the author wants you to know about Lindsay?

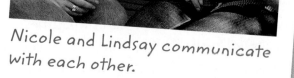

Nicole and Lindsay communicate with each other.

baseball...want...play...

To demonstrate this, Lindsay explains how in English a person might ask *Do you want to play baseball?* She models how interpreters using ASL would raise their eyebrows to show that a question is coming and then would sign *Baseball want play?*

When she was mainstreamed, Lindsay liked being with hearing friends. She remembers, "A lot of my classmates were eager to learn signs. It was really wonderful how I became socialized in the hearing world."

Lindsay admits that there were times when having an interpreter was annoying and stressful. "Sometimes when I wanted to have a conversation with friends the interpreters would stare at me. I felt like I had no privacy." She continues, "Yes, sometimes it's cool to have an interpreter, but there are those times when it got on my nerves!"

When Lindsay was ready for high school, she decided to attend a public school with a program for the Deaf. She confesses, "When I started to hang out with deaf people, I realized how much easier it is to communicate in my first language (ASL)."

Lindsay admits that she can't imagine working as a sign language interpreter. "It sounds like such a boring job, to repeat every word. But that is probably because ASL is my first language. I could see interpreters enjoying using ASL when it is not their first language."

What About You?

Would you like to be a sign language interpreter? If you like working with people and would like to learn American Sign Language, you might be a good candidate. If there are deaf students at your school, you might consider starting a club to learn ASL. Then you can begin to sign with your friends. Who knows, it might even come in handy in your next baseball game! ◯

> After reading the article, what are two important ideas to remember? Why do you think that?

Hello

What a Job!

Based on what you've read about ASL interpreters, what are the benefits of this job? Would this job suit your interests, abilities, and personality? Write a letter to a friend explaining why you would or would not like to work as a sign language interpreter.

Sign Language Interpreters

List places you have observed sign language interpreters. If you've never seen any, list some places where their skills might be helpful. Then write a sentence or two explaining why interpreters are needed in each of these places.

No

Yes

It's Language

Do you know any of the signals used by umpires, referees, or players in baseball, football, soccer, or another sport? Do you know any of the signals that a conductor uses to lead a band or orchestra? Make a list of several signals or signs used in sports or music and tell what they mean. You may want to illustrate each signal or sign.

RIBBIT

Story Code

Write a simple story on any topic you wish. Within your story, hide a secret message. Perhaps your message appears if you write the first letter of the word that starts each line of the story. Perhaps it shows up if you write every tenth word of the story. You decide. Once you write your story, see how long it takes a reader to find the hidden message.

Neigh Means "Yes"

Animals as well as people communicate. Choose an animal that interests you and find out all you can about how it communicates. Use this information to write an acrostic poem about the animal.

Nifty Fifty

Did you know that Theodor Seuss Geisel wrote *Green Eggs and Ham* on a dare from his editor? The challenge was to write a book using only 50 different words. Find a copy of this book and read it. Make a list of the 50 words used throughout the book. Then read a recent story you have written and list the different words you used. How many were there? You may want to accept the editor's challenge and try writing a 50-word story of your own.

More Books

Ellerbusch, Kristin. *Talk with Your Hands, Listen with Your Eyes*. Child's World, 1993.

Fain, Kathleen. *Handsigns: A Sign Language Alphabet*. Chronicle, 1993.

Hunter, Sara Hoagland. *The Unbreakable Code*. Northland, 1996.

Janeczko, Paul. *Loads of Codes and Secret Ciphers*. Macmillan, 1994.

Kerby, Mona. *Samuel Morse*. F. Watts, 1991.

Quackenbush, Robert M. *Quick, Annie, Give Me a Catchy Line: A Story of Samuel F.B. Morse*. Prentice-Hall, 1983.

Schwartz, Alvin. *The Cat's Elbow and Other Secret Languages*. Farrar Straus Giroux, 1982.

On the Web

Morse Code
http://www.morsehistoricsite.org
http://www.morsum.demon.co.uk/links.html

Navajo Code Talkers
http://www.history.navy.mil/faqs/
    faq61-2.htm

Sign Language
http://www.handspeak.com
http://commtechlab.msu.edu/sites/aslweb/
http://www.where.com

Across the Curriculum

Social Studies

Sign language interpreters are not the only translators who have challenging jobs. Translators at the United Nations have some of the most difficult translation jobs of all. They translate important speeches at the very moment they hear the words. If they make mistakes, big problems can result. Make a list of the kinds of training and personal qualities that you think a United Nations translator would need. Then use this list to write a job ad for the classified advertising section of a newspaper.

Art

Invent some symbols for your classroom. For example, lips with a finger in front of them could stand for "quiet." Arms raised in a cheer could mean "good job." Draw the symbols on poster board. Use bright colors and make them large enough to be visible to everyone in the classroom.

The Tap Code

During the Vietnam Conflict, thousands of American soldiers were taken prisoner. These prisoners of war (POWs) knew that communication was often the key to survival in the prison camps. By communicating, POWs could support each other through some horrible times.

In the North Vietnamese prison camps, there were strict rules against communication. There was no talking allowed between prisoners at any time or in any place. Four POWs, Capt. Carlyle Harris, Lt. Phillip Butler, Lt. Robert Peel, and Lt. Com. Robert Shumaker, came up with a secret code to get around this no-talking rule. They taught their simple code to other POWs. Eventually American prisoners in all of the Vietnamese prisons knew and were communicating with the Tap Code.

The Tap Code was based on a five-by-five alphabet grid. Each letter had a row number and a column number. (The letters *c* and *k* were the same.) The prisoners used two sets of taps for each letter—the row number, followed by a pause, and then the column number. For example, the letter *b* was tap, pause, tap, tap. There were two pauses between letters.

POWs found that they could tap on anything and communicate. They tapped on rice bowls, cell doors and walls, and water pipes. They also could sweep, cough, snap towels, and blink their eyes in Tap Code. When some prisoners were on clean-up duty, they would bang dishes and pots and pans together in Tap Code. All of this tapping made some prisons sound like dens of woodpeckers!

The POWs also came up with abbreviations. This saved time when passing messages. *GN* was used for "Good night." The usual reply was *ST* (sleep tight) and was sometimes followed by *DLTBBB* (don't let the bed bugs bite).

Taps	1	2	3	4	5
1	A	B	C, K	D	E
2	F	G	H	I	J
3	L	M	N	O	P
4	Q	R	S	T	U
5	V	W	X	Y	Z

The Tap Code was better for the POWs than Morse code because dashes could not be tapped.

TAP
TAP
TAP

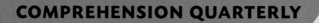

COMPREHENSION QUARTERLY

CQ⁴

ISSUE B: Determining
Important Ideas and Themes

Rest and Relaxation

THINK ABOUT: Determining Important Ideas and Themes

B4

NONFICTION
It's Just Fun and Games!
Did you know that jump rope was once a boys-only game? Read to find out about the history of string games, Mancala, and much more.

B11

FICTION
A Wild Roller Coaster Ride
Find out what Jenny and her friends have in store as they ride The Rockin' Roller Coaster.

B19

NONFICTION
Soothe Your Senses
How do you relax after a long day? Read to find out how you can soothe your senses.

B25

FICTION
The Trap
Izumi goes camping with his family, but there are some mysterious happenings in their camp.

DETERMINING IMPORTANT IDEAS AND THEMES

Go Fly a Kite!

Sometimes we read a book for specific information. However, it's easy to get carried away by all the details and what's important to us. To help us **determine the most important ideas or themes,** we need to classify and rank information.

The following article has information about kites. Joe wants to learn how to choose a kite. Read the article and Joe's thinking as he looks for answers to his questions.

"Go fly a kite!" you might say to an annoying brother, hoping he'll go away. "Great idea!" he might reply. Kites may be among the oldest toys on the planet, but they are still a favorite pastime.

Kites can be simple, homemade toys or technical—and expensive—creations. All kites have a framework covered with paper, cloth, or other material.

If you are just learning to fly a kite, choose one that you can afford. Your first kite will probably end up with a few rips.

> This stuff is interesting, but there's nothing here about choosing a kite.

> I should buy a kite that I can afford.

When you have more kite-flying experience, upgrade to a more expensive kite. Be sure your kite will be suitable for the wind conditions in your area. A more expensive, sturdier kite is better for a windy area. Be aware: small kites fly well and are easy to learn with. Big kites pull harder and are more exciting to fly.

If your kite flies too fast, then add a tail to it to slow it down . . .

> The information that smaller kites are easier to learn with, is important to me, since I'm just learning.

> I don't know if I need a tail yet, so this information isn't as important right now.

After reading the article, Joe came up with the following checklist to bring with him when he goes kite shopping.

By classifying and ranking information in the text, Joe was able to get just what he wanted out of the article. Try this technique as you read the next article about games.

Affordable
Suitable for wind conditions
Small—easy to fly

It's Just Fun and Games!

by Carol Hosking

Imagine a time when there were no TVs or computers. No skateboards or scooters. Children had to make their own fun. And, as often as not, that meant they played games.

Chances are, these were the same games that their parents played—and their parents before them. Many games, in fact, go back to the bustling wharves of ancient Egypt or to the cobblestone streets of Rome. Sailors, soldiers, and settlers took these games wherever they went—and then children taught them to each other.

That part hasn't changed! Children are still showing other children how to play games on sidewalks, on playgrounds, and on computers. So what's kept the ball rolling? It's simple: games are fun!

Mancala

The "newest" game might actually be the oldest game in the world! We know that Mancala was conceived and played in the Middle East and parts of Asia at least 3,500 years ago.

Historians believe Mancala-like boards were probably used as an accounting system in Mesopotamia and ancient Egypt to keep track of traded goods. Historians have even found similar-looking game boards carved into the roof slabs of Egyptian temples. Mancala's popularity has rocketed through centuries and across borders. Today it is among the top five board games in the world!

To play Mancala, you need some holes in the ground and some pebbles or seeds. Go one better, if you wish, with a modified egg

This Mancala board has 2 ranks and 14 bins.

carton or a professional board. Now that you're ready to play, you'll find that there are many variations of the game. There might be two, three, or four "ranks" (rows) of "bins" (holes) on the board. The number of bins might vary, too, as might the number of seeds, marbles, or stones used in the game.

What are some of the details you have learned about Mancala?

For detailed rules, check out the Internet, library books, or ask a friend. Then find a partner, dig some holes, gather pebbles, and give Mancala a try.

Jump Rope

Hey, don't skip over this one, guys. Jump rope was once a boys-only game! Girls weren't even allowed to play, in case they got hurt!

Gradually, girls *did* join the fun, but there were differences in how girls and boys played the game. Girls made up oodles of jumping rhymes—and were careful not to let their ankles show. Boys went in for tricky jumps that showed off their skill and quickness.

Long before the first "Teddy bear, teddy bear . . . " however, jumping rope flourished in ancient Egypt and China. Here, rope was needed for transportation and trade, so the harbors bustled with rope-makers jumping over long strands of hemp. Children picked up the leftover rope and soon got to jumping themselves. This curious game attracted the attention of visitors to the ports, who took the idea back to their homelands. Eventually it reached the American Colonies, and before long, it seemed like the whole world was jumping!

Some girls like to make up rhymes when they jump rope. These girls are having a ball at a May Day party.

String Games

String games have been passed on for many generations throughout the world. Traditionally, string figures were used in storytelling. Elders spun "pictures" with the string as they spun tales. Their stories and string figures often described things in everyday life, such as a star, a fish, a mosquito, or a wolf. Although many of the same patterns are found throughout the world, storytellers give them different names, depending on where they live.

String figures of reindeer and woolly mammoths, for example, are part of the Alaskan Inuit culture. Native American storytellers have passed down figures of coyotes, buffalo, frogs, and arrows. And Hawaiians continue to weave "hei" (meaning "to snare") figures such as fish and hammocks. There are snakes, lizards, and birds in South American string games; butterflies in Japan; bats in Africa; and palm trees in Australia.

You've probably already played Cat's Cradle. Find one of the many Web sites or books on string games and try your hands at Cup and Saucer, Crow's Feet, Cat's Whiskers, and the awesome Jacob's Ladder.

Once you're an expert, you can make up your own string stories or figures and share them with your family and friends.

> What is the main idea behind string games?

Marbles

There's always a game in your pocket if you have a few marbles and at least one friend. When you think about it, sticks and stones might have been the first sporting equipment around. Many of today's target sports and lawn games go back to using those very objects.

Every year the National Marbles Tournament is held in Wildwood, New Jersey, for the best players under fifteen years old.

Playing with marbles is *really* playing with history. Marbles have been found in the ruins of ancient Egyptian, Aztec, and prehistoric Mound Builder and Pueblo cultures!

The earliest marbles were pebbles rounded by the ocean, fruit pits, and nuts. Modern ones are made of marble, glass, plastic, and even steel ball bearings. In parts of the Middle East, children play with baked clay marbles or sheep knucklebones. And at Passover, Jewish children play marbles with hazelnuts.

Basically, the object is to roll, drop, or throw your marbles against your opponents' marbles in order to knock them out of a circle. But settle this first: will the game be "for keeps" (winner keeps all the marbles, loser weeps) or "for fair" (your marbles go back in your pocket at the end of the game)?

What is one thing you need to remember when playing marbles?

checkers

Some historians say that George Washington enjoyed a game of checkers now and then. Was he just relaxing or was he planning his next strategy at Valley Forge or the White House?

One form or another of checkers has been a popular "brain game" since the days of the pharaohs. This game showed up in paintings, inscriptions, and pottery of ancient Egypt. As with Mancala boards, checkerboards have been found carved into roofs in early Egyptian temples. Originally the game was played on a five-by-five square board and was called Alquerque. It soon spread throughout the world, eventually making its way to Europe when the Moors invaded Spain in the 700s. About 300 years later, probably in France, people switched from playing the game on an Alquerque

Throughout its history, checkers has had a variety of names and forms. This English version was called Draughts.

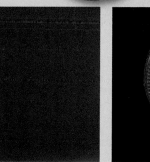

board to a chessboard. Among other things, this meant that there were now eight-by-eight squares. Players could now spread out their pieces and increase the playing field.

The new format went through a variety of names and rules, including Jeu Force, a version that forces a player to take his opponent whenever possible. This soon became Draughts (pronounced "drafts") in England and Scotland. And from there, it was only a hop, skip, and a jump away to becoming our own familiar game of checkers.

Hopscotch

With only a stone and a piece of chalk, you can hop till you drop.

Archaeologists have found hopscotch grids carved into the cobblestones of ancient Rome. Later, Roman soldiers laid out similar, but much bigger, grids in Britain to exercise their armies. (The troops trained by running through the long courses, wearing full armor and backpacks.)

Centuries later, hopscotch was a welcome game enjoyed by the American Colonists. Folks took time off from the intense chores of barn raising and planting crops to play games and have fun. While the adults engaged in footraces, plowing contests, and charades, children played hopscotch, leapfrog, and London Bridge.

Don't lose your balance or step on a chalk line.

Hopscotch "boards" and rules change all the time, but the way it's played is simple. Just draw a grid on the sidewalk, toss your marker, and hop to one end and back again. Of course there are a few rules—you miss a turn if you lose your balance, step on a line, or skip a square.

As the expression goes, the more things change, the more they stay the same. And this can certainly be said of all these games. Nothing much seems to change, except the children who play them.

So it's up to you to keep the ball rolling. You can always hang out at the mall, play video games, park yourself in front of the TV, or talk on the phone, but why not seize this opportunity for a change of pace? Play a game!

What main idea was the author trying to get across in this article?

Write the Rule Book

What's your favorite game? Write the rules so that a second-grade student could understand them. Include information about materials needed to play the game, scoring, and winning. Then use your rules as you teach someone to play.

Family Game Night

Write a letter to your parents convincing them to start a family game night at home. In your letter, include reasons why playing board games would bring your family closer together. Ask your parents for their opinions about how often to schedule the game night and what snacks might be served. Share the finished letter with your parents.

The Name of the Game

In a small group, make up a new game that uses simple materials. Practice playing the game and make adjustments to your rules as needed. Come up with a catchy name for your game. When you're ready, demonstrate the game to the class.

MAKE YOUR OWN DREAM CATCHER

Many Native Americans hang a dream catcher above their beds to sift out their good and bad dreams. The Lakota people created the dream catcher, a willow hoop decorated with feathers and beads. According to Lakota legend, the hole in the center of a dream catcher lets only good dreams reach the sleeper. The web on a dream catcher traps bad dreams until they disappear in daylight. With a few supplies from your local craft store, you can make your own dream catcher to hang in your room. Sweet dreams!

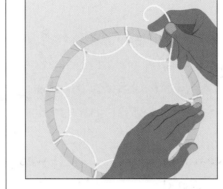

What you'll need:

5" metal or wooden ring
4 yards of suede lacing
3 yards of 1/8-inch waxed nylon string
1 small conch or seashell with a hole in it
About 25 beads in assorted colors
Feathers
A clothespin or large paper clip
Glue

Here's what to do:

1. Cut an 8-foot piece of the suede lacing. Glue one end of the suede to the ring. Wrap the suede around the ring until it has gone all the way around it. Glue the end of the suede lacing to the ring. Hold the lacing in place with a clothespin or paper clip until the glue dries.

2. To make the web, tie one end of the nylon string to the ring. Make nine hitch knots around the ring, spacing them about 1-1/2" apart (see the illustration above).

3. Begin the next row of the web in the middle of the thread that you have already woven on Row 1. Continue weaving around and around until you have just a small hole left in the center. Tie a knot in the thread and add a tiny

drop of glue to the knot. When the glue has dried, cut off the extra thread.

4. Attach the small shell to the top middle of the ring with an 8-inch piece of the lacing. Divide the remaining lacing into eight 10-inch pieces and tie them to the bottom, sides, and center of the dream catcher. Slip beads onto each piece of lacing.

5. Push two feathers up inside the beads on each piece of lacing. Glue the feathers if they are loose. If you still have feathers left, attach them to each side of the shell.

6. Use the remaining lacing to make a loop for hanging your dream catcher. Sweet dreams!

A Wild Roller Coaster Ride
by Elaine Kule

"**I** can't believe you'll be ten years old next week," Jenny's brother, Tony, said during dinner. "My baby sister," he said with a sigh. He was twelve.

"What do you want for your birthday?" their father asked.

"You can have anything you like, honey," Mom said. "Well, almost anything," she said with a wink.

"What I want isn't a thing, it's a place," Jenny said. "I'd like to go to the amusement park with Lee, Joey, and Teena. There's a new roller coaster ride that's supposed to be really scary. Will you take us? Please!"

Lee, Joey, and Teena were Jenny's best friends. They did nearly everything together.

"Since when do you like being scared?" Tony asked. "You almost cried at the last scary movie we saw."

"I was younger then," Jenny said. "So, what do you think, Mom and Dad? Can we go to the amusement park?"

"Well, since your birthday's on a Sunday this year, maybe Dad and I can arrange the trip," Mrs. Santos said. "I'll call your friends' parents to see if it's OK with them."

"Thanks!" Jenny said. She was so excited she could hardly eat.

Her friends were thrilled about the trip. Their parents thought the amusement park was a great way to spend a birthday, and they all agreed to the idea.

What important piece of information did we learn from Tony about Jenny? Why might this detail be important to know?

"We're going to have so much fun!" Teena said during math club.

"I can't wait," said Joey. He was Teena's twin brother, although they didn't look alike. "I hear that the new roller coaster is terrific."

Jenny nodded happily. At home, she marked the days until her birthday on a small calendar. She even hummed the birthday song while cleaning her room.

Finally, Sunday arrived. By 11:00 that morning, Jenny was at the park with her family and friends. She skipped through the entrance gate, her eyes dancing with joy. There was so much to see, Jenny didn't know where to look first. The games, the rides, the brightly colored lights, the good things to eat—everything looked wonderful.

After singing "Happy Birthday" to Jenny over wads of cotton candy, the group headed for the roller coaster. Jenny and her friends had to stand against a cardboard clown whose hand was raised four and one-half feet from the ground. A sign read: "You must be this tall to ride The Rockin' Roller Coaster." Luckily, the four children passed the test.

While standing in line, they watched the roller coaster complete its frightening run of twists and turns. Screams and laughter filled the air. "Are you children sure you want to go through with this?" Mr. Santos asked, looking up at the huge ride. "It's not too late to back out."

"No way, sir," Lee said with a grin. "This is going to be great!"

When the roller coaster came to a stop, its passengers stumbled out. Some looked a bit shaken. A few were giggling. Jenny and her friends barely noticed, though. They scrambled into seats and strapped themselves into safety harnesses. Jenny helped Lee with hers.

What seems to be the most important event in Jenny's life right now? Why do you think so?

They waited excitedly for the other riders to settle in. Then, with a lurch, the roller coaster moved forward. Slowly at first, they rode along the curved track. Jenny tightly gripped the harness around her. Any minute now, they'd be flying through space. At least it would feel that way.

Sure enough, the roller coaster picked up speed. It moved so fast that the ground below was a blur. The car twirled this way and that. It climbed toward the clouds, then dropped straight down. Jenny knew that most of the screams she heard were coming from her own mouth. Maybe this wasn't such a good idea after all, she thought.

They entered a tunnel. "Oh no," Jenny whispered, as a curtain of darkness fell over the car. She didn't like tunnels very much. But in seconds, they were outside again.

"Thank goodness," Jenny said softly. She looked at Lee. A river of tears streamed down her friend's face.

Suddenly, the roller coaster came to a halt. Jenny looked around. They'd landed all right, but it wasn't on Earth. Across the sky was a brilliant rainbow. Bright jewels lined the streets. And standing in front of the roller coaster was the oddest-looking creature Jenny had ever seen. She had purple skin, green hair, and wore a shiny gold dress.

"What's going on?" Lee asked.

"Where are we?" Joey wanted to know.

Jenny turned and saw the other passengers sitting stiffly in their seats, staring straight ahead as though they were frozen in time.

When the creature pointed at Jenny with a crablike finger, the girl nearly fainted. "You, please rise," it said in a squeaky voice.

"Better do as she says," Teena whispered.

With trembling hands, Jenny unfastened her safety harness and slowly stood. In a flash, she was lifted from the roller coaster and flown to the creature. She couldn't believe it.

"Humans love that little trick," the creature said. "Look, kid, here's the deal. We need someone to be Queen of Niceland. We want a good person. A rose without thorns, you might say. We think you'd be perfect for the job. And you can have your friends stay here with you. How about it? It's your choice."

"Why us?" Jenny asked. "And why now?"

"We've been watching you," the creature said. "You seem like good kids. And as everyone knows, children make the best rulers. As for your second question, we can only bring humans here when one of them has a birthday."

Just then a sea of creatures representing every color of the rainbow sprung out from behind the nearby trees and bushes. "You'll like it here," one of them said.

"We have ice cream in 51 flavors," said another.

"And big-screen TVs with 500 channels," added a creature who had an eye where its nose should be. "What more could anyone want?"

As good as it all sounded, Jenny knew that she had to get back to Earth. "Look, I'm sorry, but I can't stay here," she told the group. "I'd miss my family and school and math club. And I know the others agree with me. But thanks just the same."

"We understand," the first creature said. "But since it's your birthday, how about some ice cream for you and your friends? The flavor of the day is pizza."

"It sounds delicious, but we'd better get back. My parents must be worried."

Jenny was right. In fact, everyone at the amusement park was staring at the sky, wondering what could have happened to the roller coaster. Mr. Santos was calling the White House on his cell phone, hoping a spaceship could be sent up to search for the children. But then, there they were, coming right out of the sky it seemed. When the roller coaster stopped at last, Jenny was the first one out of her seat. She ran to her parents and hugged them.

"Am I glad to see you!" she said.

"We feel the same way," Mrs. Santos said, tears filling her eyes.

"What happened?" Mr. Santos asked.

"I'm not sure," Jenny said. She wasn't quite ready to talk about it. All she knew was that she'd never forget Niceland, not if she lived for 100 more birthdays.

"Well, what's next, honey?" Mrs. Santos asked her daughter.

"Can we get some pizza?" Jenny asked. Traveling to another world had made her hungry.

"Sounds good to me," Mr. Santos said smiling. Jenny saw that her parents really had been worried. She held each of their hands and swung them happily. She wouldn't trade life on Earth for even one day on Niceland. ◉

What was one important thing that you learned about Jenny in this story?

Stop and Respond

A Big Kid Now

Do you remember the first time you were tall enough to ride your favorite amusement park ride or ride around the block on your bike? Write a short poem about your experience.

The World of Niceland

The author of "A Wild Roller Coaster Ride" left a lot to the imagination with her description of Niceland and its residents. Sometimes the best part of reading a story is using your imagination to fill in the gaps. Use brightly colored markers to create a picture of Niceland as you imagine it.

Wanted: Rose with No Thorns

It's your job to fill the position of Queen of Niceland. So far you haven't had much luck. You've decided to place an ad in a popular kid's magazine. Write a classified ad that will make kids rush to interview for the job.

Follow Your Dreams

Throughout history, people have tried to figure out what their dreams mean. From famous scientists to curious individuals, many people believe that our dreams express thoughts and feelings that we may not be aware of—or don't want to think about—when we are awake.

Here are some common things that people dream about and popular theories about what they mean.

● If you dream about trees, you may be recognizing a new opportunity in your life. It could be a place on a team or a new friend waiting. Is there something new that could be awaiting you? Think carefully, then seize the moment!

● If you dream about being chased, it could mean that you are avoiding someone or something in your life. Better to face your troubles than let them get away from you.

● If you dream that you are flying, it may mean that you want to escape from some boring routines in your life. Take a day off from your routine when you can— plan a long bike ride, read an exciting book, play some ball, have a sleepover, or enjoy the outdoors.

● If you dream about a tornado, ask yourself if something in your life has suddenly changed. You might want to talk about this change with a friend or family member, or write about it in your diary.

● If your dreams involve certain people, they can provide clues about the way you think about yourself. Maybe there's something you would like to change about yourself or qualities or characteristics you admire about the person in your dreams that you would like to have.

So the next time you have a vivid dream, write about it in your journal. What do you think it might be trying to tell you?

DETERMINING IMPORTANT IDEAS AND THEMES

The Beach

Often we read something that is so full of great images or information, we become confused as to what is the important idea or theme the writer is trying to get across to us. So we ask ourselves, "What *must* I remember about what I've read? What are the important ideas that the author wants me to understand?" **To determine important ideas and themes** in what you read, it's helpful to identify the main idea and the details that support those main ideas.

One way to do this is to create a two-column chart like the one Paulina did below. On the left side of the chart, she listed the main idea of what she had read. On the right side, she listed the details that supported the main idea. Read the example below.

Whenever the pressures of living up to her mother's expectations made Leah hunch up her shoulders, snap at her baby brother, or feel as if she were wearing a very tight swimming cap, Leah knew it was time to head to the beach. For Leah, the beach was the perfect place to relax. When she walked along the shore, her troubles melted away with each gently crashing wave. The screeching of the gulls drowned out memories of her mother's nagging about homework. The cool, wet stones massaged Leah's feet, which were aching from hours and hours of ballet practice. And the gentle breeze reminded her to breathe slowly, expelling her negative thoughts one at a time as she exhaled.

Main Idea	Supporting Details
Leah went to the beach to relax.	The crashing waves melted her troubles away.
	She forgot about her mom's nagging when the gulls screeched.
	The cool, wet stones felt good on her feet.
	The gentle breeze helped her to breathe easily.

As you read the next article, "Soothe your Senses," use a chart like the one above to keep track of the main ideas and details in it.

SOOTHE YOUR *Senses*

by June Hetzel

*H*ave you ever felt tense or "keyed up" about something?
I'm sure you have. When you feel tense, it's important to find ways
to relax. Nature gives us five ways to experience the world around
us—sight, sound, touch, smell, and taste. Through our senses, we
enjoy natural ways to relax and enjoy our world. Let's go!

Touch

Think back to a time when you visited an ocean or a large lake. Remember the feeling of the cool water as the waves lapped at your feet? Remember the texture of the sand as you walked barefoot along the beach? Relive that moment in your mind. What were you thinking? How were you feeling? Record your thoughts in your journal.

Some people love to be in the water. Think back to a time when you took a long, hot bubble bath or perhaps stood underneath the stream of water from the showerhead. Did you feel more or less relaxed after your bath or shower? Why do you think you felt that way?

FACT: Hot baths and showers naturally relax you. The warm water relieves tired muscles.

FACT: People even pay as much as $40 for a bath—a mineral bath, that is! Mineral baths are believed to have benefits for arthritis, a disease that makes your joints feel achy.

FACT: Bath, England, and Calistoga, California, are famous for their natural hot springs. People travel far and wide to visit these cities. They plan whole vacations around taking baths!

FACT: Mineral and mud baths go back hundreds of years. Hot baths soothe aches, improve blood flow, and cleanse the skin. The texture and the warmth naturally soothe you.

> After reading this section, what type of experience did the author stress as relaxing?

Sound

With a flick of a switch, we can make a room come alive with music. But we don't always have to create sounds. Sometimes they're all around us. Listen to all the sounds in the room. Record the sounds you hear on a piece of paper. Now, with your teacher's permission, open a window or step outside for a few minutes. Listen to the sounds. Write down whatever you hear. Now go back and circle the sounds that are relaxing to you.

FACT: The sounds of ocean waves, a trickling stream, falling leaves, or the whistling of a songbird can all help people naturally relax.

FACT: Many adults purchase small water fountains to set on a desk in their offices. The fountains have water trickling over rocks. The sound reminds them of a trickling creek. The fountains duplicate nature's natural way of relaxing us.

FACT: People who live in cities experience extra stress caused by noise. Honking horns, planes flying overhead, traffic jams, loud subways—all these are examples of stressful noise. Find a safe, quiet place in or near where you live. With an adult's permission, go to this place and enjoy the peaceful sounds of nature. Consider taking a good book to read or your journal to write in.

Smell

When was the last time you smelled a wonderful bouquet of flowers? What did you feel as you inhaled the flowers' scent?

Or think back to a time when you smelled something wonderful cooking for dinner. What kinds of smells make you happy? What smells do you say "yuck" to? Record your thoughts in your journal.

FACT: Aromatherapy uses smells to relax people. Lavender is a favorite aroma known for its calming effects, and that's why many people enjoy lavender lotions and bubble baths! Mulling spices are another favorite use of smells. Spices are heated with water on the stove, and the soothing aromas of cinnamon, nutmeg, and other simmering favorites fill the house.

FACT: Smells can make you more alert and learn better! The smell of lemon and the smell of peppermint have both been known to help increase alertness.

FACT: In some countries, they use smells in museums to help people remember and enjoy their experiences. For example, if you visit the Jorvik Viking Centre in York, England, you'll feel like you're

experiencing Viking days. As you sit in a small car and ride through the barnyard, you'll notice that it smells like pigs and chickens! Yuck! Or, on the more pleasant side, if you walk through the Calderdale Industrial Museum in England, you'll enjoy the wonderful aroma of butterscotch candies being sprayed from a small pipe overhead.

FACT: Nature uses good smells to relax you and stinky smells to warn you. For example, the stink bug and the skunk both use foul odors to warn their enemies!

What is one important idea that you have learned about relaxing smells?

Taste

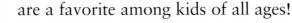

What are your favorite foods? Many people enjoy fresh fruits because of their refreshing flavors and juices. Vegetables are another favorite because of their low-calorie crunch. Of course, warm cookies are a favorite among kids of all ages!

What are your favorite meals cooked by your parents or grandparents? What kinds of foods do you like to eat when you aren't feeling well? Are your favorite foods salty, sweet, sour, or bitter? Take a few moments to jot down your food lists and share some of your favorites with a friend. Why do these foods make you feel so good?

FACT: Some food is considered "comfort food" for the psychological comfort it gives us. Sometimes the food is a favorite because it's served to us by a special person, such as Mom or Dad, and holds special memories. Foods like chicken soup or mashed potatoes are common "comfort foods."

FACT: The steam and spices from chicken soup clear a stuffy nose, and the liquid helps keep up your body fluids—not to mention that the soup has a delicious flavor.

FACT: Eat regularly to keep your energy high. Don't skip meals. Limit sugars and eat natural foods. Eat fruits and vegetables—they have antioxidants. Antioxidants help fight illness and keep you well.

FACT: Try a warm glass of milk or a slice of turkey before you go to bed—they'll help you relax and go to sleep. Milk and turkey have an amino acid in them called *tryptophan*. Tryptophan triggers the brain chemical, serotonin, which is believed to help you feel sleepy.

FACT: When you have a sore throat, swallow a spoonful of honey with a little lemon squeezed on top. The honey will coat and soothe your throat. The lemon stimulates your salivary glands, making your mouth water, which makes it easier to swallow.

Sight

Stop reading for a moment and look around you. What colors do you see that you like? What is your favorite color? How does this color make you feel? Have you ever seen a sunset that seemed to paint the sky with red and orange? If you could decorate your room any color, what color would you choose? Why?

Look at the photographs below. If you could step into any one of these scenes, which would you step into, and why? Did the color affect your choice? How?

FACT: Bright colors increase alertness. Red and yellow "wake" people up! This is why classrooms and nurseries are often decorated with bright colors, and why emergency vehicles are bright red!

FACT: Muted colors, like soft pinks, blues, and greens, can calm people. This is why some hospital rooms are painted with muted tones. Some people like muted tones in their homes because they feel peaceful when they're surrounded by calm colors.

FACT: Your eyes can become tired if you do too much close-up work. When you are reading and writing, look up now and then and look as far into the distance as you can. That will relax your eyes— and at the same time, you can enjoy all the beauty around you.

We experience our world through touch, sound, taste, smell, and sight. Through our senses, nature gives us many ways to naturally relax and enjoy the world. Take time to touch, hear, smell, taste, and see the beauty in the world. Soothe your senses! ●

What was the most important thing you learned from this article?

Stop and Respond

RECIPE FOR Relaxation

When you're tense and worried about something, it helps to have a "recipe" for relaxation—that is, a list of surefire tricks to help you relax. Using the ideas in the article, put together a list of sights, sounds, smells, and tastes that are guaranteed to help you unwind. Keep the list in your room and consult it the next time you feel stressed-out.

Comfort IN A BOX

What's your favorite "comfort food"? Is it mashed potatoes smothered with gravy? your mom's chocolate chip cookies? or gooey macaroni and cheese? Create a class menu for a restaurant that serves all these comfort foods. Be sure to write a descriptive phrase for each item on the menu so your "customers" know what they're ordering.

SIGHTS FOR Sore Eyes

Gather some old magazines and search through them for images of peaceful scenes. On a large piece of poster board, create a collage out of your images. If you want, also include words from the magazine that have a calming effect on you.

The Trap

by Mike Graf

"Where are the marshmallows?" nine-year-old Izumi asked.

"I put them on the top shelf," his father answered, poking the logs in the fire with a stick.

"I already looked there," Izumi replied.

Izumi's seven-year-old sister, Eriko, trotted over. "Let me look." She grabbed Izumi's flashlight. "Hey, the graham crackers are gone!"

The children's mother looked up from her book. "How can you think about food? We just got back from dinner!"

"I want some chocolate chip cookies," twelve-year-old Kiyoshi announced. He hopped out of his chair and walked over to join Izumi and Eriko. The three children searched through the shelves of the tall wooden cupboard. They even looked in the family's ice chest.

After the children looked for a few more minutes, Mom announced, "You know, it's 9:30. We should be brushing our teeth and getting ready for bed."

"OK," Kiyoshi sighed.

"All right," Eriko answered. She walked back to the campfire, plopped down on her mother's lap, and watched her father pour water over the hot coals.

But Izumi continued searching. At the back of the top shelf, he found an opened box of chocolate bars. The box had been sealed less than an hour ago. As Izumi inspected the

How might the missing food be an important piece of information in this story?

candy, he felt a hand on his shoulder. He looked up and saw his father.

"We're all going over to the bathroom to brush our teeth," his dad said.

"Look at these candy bars, Dad."

"No more food for now," Dad reminded Izumi, as he walked away.

Izumi put the chocolate back and joined his family.

The next night, after a long day of fishing, the family went out to dinner— again! It was 9:30 P.M. when they left the pizza parlor. Mom and Dad said that was the last time they could eat out.

While his family got ready for the nightly trek to the bathroom, Izumi grabbed a flashlight and walked over to the cupboard. The door was unlatched and there was a box of cereal on the ground.

"Who did this?" Izumi shouted to his family, but they'd already left. He pulled out an opened bag of marshmallows. Hmmm, Izumi thought. I bet Kiyoshi's been getting into the food and leaving things a mess.

Izumi carried the bag of marshmallows to the picnic table. He got his backpack from the tent, found a marking pen, a roll of tape, and a sheet of paper. Then he wrote:

What clues might be important to solving the mystery of the missing food?

Kiyoshi: Don't eat all of these marshmallows. They're for everyone!

Izumi taped the note on the marshmallow bag and put it away. He was closing the cupboard when his mother asked, "What are you doing?"

"I'm just looking for my toothbrush," Izumi answered. He grabbed his bathroom kit and walked off.

After Izumi came back, his mother and father were already in their tent with Eriko. Kiyoshi was in his own tent.

"I'll show him!" Izumi snickered. He grabbed a small broom and smoothed out the dirt around the picnic table. He threaded clothesline through several pots and pans and tied the rope between two trees, directly in the path between Kiyoshi's tent and the cupboard. "This will prove who's been taking our food."

Izumi walked over to his parents' tent and whispered goodnight, then strutted over to Kiyoshi's tent and shouted, "Goodnight, Kiyoshi!"

"Goodnight, Izumi!" Kiyoshi answered.

Izumi climbed into his own tent, slid into his sleeping bag, and fell asleep.

CRASH! BANG! CLATTER! Izumi shot up in his sleeping bag. THUMP! CRACK! RATTLE! CRASH! THUMP! Pots and pans banged and bags crackled. Wide-eyed, Izumi unzipped the tent and stepped out. It was too dark to see, so he listened silently. After more rattling, he heard the heavy thumping of footsteps coming toward him. He quickly scampered back into the safe arms of his tent and zipped up the flap. "Kiyoshi!" Izumi whispered, but there was no answer. "Kiyoshi," Izumi said louder, "is that you?" Izumi pulled his sleeping bag up to his neck, his heart pounding wildly in his chest. The footsteps grew louder; then right outside his tent, branches snapped and pine needles crunched on the ground. Izumi waited, expecting to hear Kiyoshi unzip his tent, but it soon became quiet. Izumi lay in his sleeping bag, wondering who was out there. Eventually he fell back asleep.

The next thing Izumi knew, it was morning. Remembering the traps he had set and the noises he had heard during the night, Izumi flew out of his sleeping bag, pulled on his clothes, and hopped outside. No one else was up.

Right outside his tent, Izumi picked up the marshmallow bag with the note still attached. The bag was ripped and only two marshmallows were left. "It *was* Kiyoshi!" Izumi muttered to himself.

Izumi looked up. "Oh no!" There were pieces of bread, half-eaten apples, a broken jar of peanut butter, and a box of cereal that was ripped to shreds. The ice chest was tipped over by the road. Next to it was a carton of spilled milk, empty yogurt cups, torn cheese wrappers, and broken egg shells. Izumi also noticed that the rope was ripped from the tree and pots and pans were lying everywhere.

There were dozens of footprints where Izumi had swept the dirt. He noticed that some were from an animal and some were from shoes. Izumi crept over to Kiyoshi's tent and grabbed one of his brother's sneakers. He stepped back to the footprints and bent down to press Kiyoshi's shoe into the dirt next to one of the prints. His shoe was too small. Izumi stood up slowly and gulped. "It wasn't Kiyoshi. But if it wasn't him, then who was it?"

Izumi's mother unzipped her tent, looked out, and yawned. "Why are you up so early?"

"Mom! You have to come out here!" Izumi pleaded.

"Why?" his father asked, peering outside.

"Someone was in our camp last night!" Izumi explained.

His mom and dad quickly came outside, still wearing their pajamas. Kiyoshi and Eriko were right behind them.

Mom looked around, then asked, "What happened?"

Izumi explained. "Last night before I went to bed, I set up some traps to catch Kiyoshi because I thought he was getting into our food."

"Me?" Kiyoshi questioned.

Izumi continued. "I taped this note to the marshmallow bag. I also strung up the pots and pans and smoothed out the dirt for footprints. During the middle of the night, I woke up and heard noises outside and thought it was Kiyoshi.

"Noises, huh?" Dad said, as he looked around at his family.

"Yes, crashing and banging," Izumi replied. "When I got up this morning and saw the footprints, I checked them with Kiyoshi's shoes. They weren't his!"

"You're right . . ." Dad started to say. He stamped the sole of his slipper into the dirt, right next to one of the prints left during the night, and then he looked up.

"Dad!" Izumi cried out. "It was you!"

Dad looked sheepish. "This fresh air is affecting my appetite. I've been really hungry."

Kiyoshi flashed a big smile at his brother.

"I'm sorry I deceived you," Dad continued. "I got up and had some cookies. Good thing I didn't trip on your rope!"

"You sure were noisy!" Izumi exclaimed.

"No, I wasn't. I didn't want to wake anybody," Dad explained. "There must have been an animal in our camp last night." He crouched down and pointed to the prints in the dirt. The family bent down next to him and studied the prints.

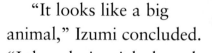

"It looks like a big animal," Izumi concluded. "I thought it might have been a dog."

Mom stood up. "Could it be a bear?"

"A bear?" Eriko asked, eyes wide open.

"Let's check and see!" Kiyoshi said. "I've got that mammal book in my tent." He ran to get the book and brought it back.

Kiyoshi thumbed to the page on bears, and the family compared the bear footprint in the book to the animal prints in the dirt.

"It's definitely a bear!" Kiyoshi proclaimed. "See how the size and shape match!"

Izumi shuddered. "A bear walked by my tent last night!"

Dad smiled. "You know what this means, don't you? It looks like we're going to have to eat out again!" ●

What important thing did you learn about camping by reading this story?

Making Tracks

Izumi's family confirmed the identity of the food thief by its tracks. What kinds of critters live in your area? Even a city has pigeons and squirrels. Grab a field guide to find pictures of the tracks made by local animals in your area. Create a poster with labeled pictures so community residents can identify area wildlife.

Do Not Feed the Bears

A bear at a campsite can be an extremely dangerous thing. At such popular camping grounds as Yellowstone National Park, officials try very hard to educate campers about the dangers of bears. For example, they suggest securing food in a tree or in the car overnight instead of leaving it unattended at a campsite. Create a pamphlet that lists five facts about bear safety.

Gather 'Round the Campfire

Camping is one of America's most popular pastimes. For many campers, telling stories around the campfire is the best part. Write a very short tale that you might share around the campfire. Your story might be scary, funny, or serious. Use lots of vivid descriptions to set the mood of your tale.

Fun and Easy as 1-2-3

What is your favorite way to relax? Share what you know about your favorite hobby with a person who has never tried it. Write step-by-step directions for your hobby. Here are some suggestions:

How to bait a hook   How to fly a kite

How to plant flowers   How to body surf

Haiku Haven

Haiku is a Japanese form of poetry that has three unrhymed lines of five, seven, and five syllables. Haiku poems are usually about nature. Write a haiku that uses descriptive details to help you remember a relaxing place you've visited. Read your haiku during times of stress.

Create a Camp

Whether you've ever been to camp or not, there are some things that are definitely required to have a good time—but those things differ from person to person. Suppose you can create whatever kind of summer camp you would like. Write a short proposal that outlines what kinds of activities you would offer at your camp, where it would be and why, what you would call it, how many kids could attend at once, what kinds of counselors you would hire, and so on. Have fun and be creative, but also try to be realistic!

Making Connections

More Books to Read

Beard, Daniel. *The American Boy's Handy Book: What to Do and How to Do It.* David R. Godine, 1998.

Meisel, Paul (Illustrator). *Games and Giggles Just for Girls.* Pleasant Company Publications, 1995.

Smith, Alistair and Nigel Reece. *The Usbourne Big Book of Paper Craft.* E.D.C. Publications, 1996.

Todd, Susan. *Boredom Blasters.* E.F. Communications, 2000.

On the Web

Sports Illustrated for Kids
http://www.sikids.com

Award-winning Books for Kids
http://www.ala.org/alsc/newbery.html

Craft Ideas
http://www.kidsdomain.com/craft/
     index.html

History of Traditional Games
http://web.ukonline.co.uk/james.masters/
     TraditionalGames

Across the Curriculum

Math
Conduct a survey of fourth graders about their favorite hobbies. Ask your classmates to list the favorite three things they do for fun. Then compute the data into percentages and create a pie chart or bar graph to show your results.

Health
Sports may seem to be all fun and games, but in order to perform your best, it's important to eat the right kinds of food. Do some research on eating a healthy diet. Prepare a short oral report, with diagrams if possible, for the class.

Catch Some zZZs

Have you ever found it difficult to get to sleep? Instead of tossing and turning, or worse—staring at the clock and fretting about not sleeping—try these tips.

- Take a nice warm shower or bath, but don't do it too soon before hitting the hay. A warm bath one to two hours before bedtime relaxes your muscles and puts you in the right frame of mind for sleep.

- Drink a glass of warm milk to relax you.

- Read a book for about a half an hour before bedtime. If you do something calming, you're more likely to fall asleep when you want to. But don't wrestle with the dog or even shower. These activities get your heart rate going, which makes it harder to sleep.

- Don't eat sugary foods or drink caffeinated pop after dinner. Sugar and caffeine are definite no-nos if you want to sleep soundly.

- Get rid of distracting noises—stick that humming alarm clock in a drawer, or close your window to block out outdoor sounds.

- Make your bedroom as comfortable as possible at bedtime. Make sure BEFORE you go to bed that you have enough blankets and that your room is not too hot or too cold.

- Do some deep-breathing exercises before you go to bed. Slow, steady breaths have a calming effect on the body.

- Count sheep! Yes, it's true. Counting things, such as breaths or imaginary sheep, helps you relax.

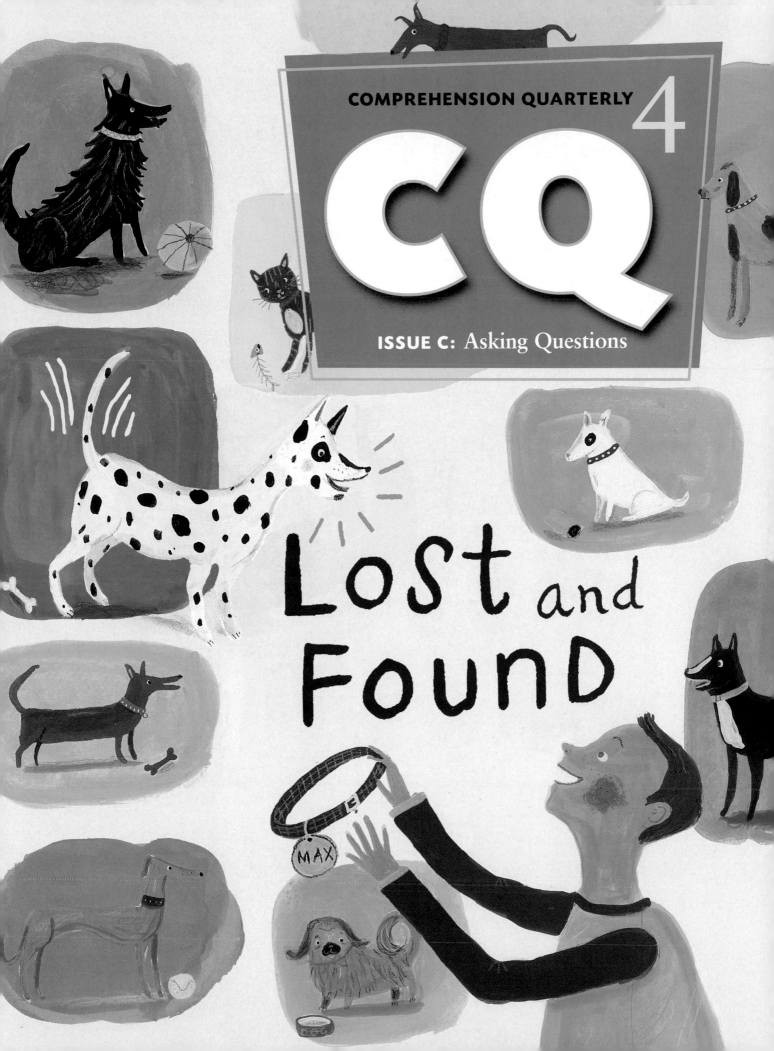

COMPREHENSION QUARTERLY

CQ 4

ISSUE C: Asking Questions

Lost and Found

Lost and Found

THINK ABOUT: Asking Questions

C4

FICTION
The Lost Jacket
There's something important in the pocket of Davy's lost jacket.

C11

NONFICTION
Pet Detectives
If you've ever lost a pet, you'll be glad these two detectives are on the job.

FICTION
Something's Out There
Is it a lost animal or something out of the pages of a history book?

C19

C24

NONFICTION
Ancient Egypt Uncovered
You can imagine losing your socks—but can you lose a whole city?

In this issue:

ASKING QUESTIONS

Lost in a Good Book

Lost on Morley Glacier sounds like a cool book, thought Carla. She pulled the book off the shelf.

Adventure books were Carla's absolute favorite thing to read. She wondered if this story would be as exciting as the title made it sound.

Carla sat at a table in the busy library. She turned the book over and read the description on the back. *Amy is separated from her family on a hike in Glacier National Park. Now dark is coming and she is alone. Will she survive the night?*

Carla thought, this sounds pretty good. I wonder if she runs into any wild animals. That would be pretty scary!

She turned to the table of contents and read the chapter titles. *Chapter 5: Danger on Two Legs.* That doesn't sound like animal trouble, she thought. Does Amy meet a dangerous person?

Soon Carla was deep into the book. It was every bit as exciting as she'd hoped it would be. As she read, Carla found herself asking some questions. She wondered if Morley Glacier was a real place. And she wondered what she would have done in Amy's place, if she had been lost and alone.

The bell rang just as Carla reached the end of Chapter 4. Carla thought ahead to the next chapter. She remembered that at the beginning of the book, Amy's family had been listening to a radio at their campsite. There had been a news alert about a bank robbery in Evergreen, not far from the park.

Carla shivered. "The bank robber! Could that be who Amy runs into?" she asked herself as she closed the book.

Like any good reader, Carla **asks all kinds of questions**—before, during, and after she reads. She previews her reading, looking for hints that tell what the text will be about. She plans how and when she will read. And she predicts what will happen in the text she hasn't read yet. Asking these kinds of questions helps Carla better understand what she reads.

Think about a book you really enjoyed reading. What did you wonder about before you started reading? How did you plan out your reading? What questions did you ask? What predictions did you make?

The Lost Jacket

by Joanne Barkan

"Here goes *everything*," Davy Gonzalez murmured. "The rest of my life depends on this." He reread the letter he had just finished writing.

Dear Aunt Mercedes and Uncle Raoul,
   I have a small favor to ask. Well, maybe not so small. Could I move back down to Florida and live with you for the next nine years? Just until I'm 18 and can join the French Foreign Legion. I hate it up here. Cold weather stinks. So does my new school. I don't know ANYONE, and I've been here a whole week. Yesterday Mom bought me long underwear. That was the last straw. I told her I'd just as soon freeze to death. Please write back before that happens.
      Your deeply desperate nephew,
      Davy

"Davy," Mom called, "you're going to be late for school."

Davy shoved the letter into an envelope. He bolted out the bedroom door and took the stairs two at a time.

"It's chilly today," Mom said. She handed him his new jacket.

Davy groaned as he pulled it on. It felt heavy. "I bet I suffocate in this," he muttered.

The jacket was red with a yellow stripe down each sleeve. Davy stuffed his letter deep into the left-hand pocket. He planned to mail it at the post office after school. He waved to his mother as he sped out the door.

Think of at least two questions you already have about Davy and the story.

Davy raced into the school building and hung his jacket on one of the pegs that lined the long hallway. He slipped into Mrs. Porter's fourth-grade classroom just as the last bell rang.

Davy tried to concentrate on what Mrs. Porter was saying about the life cycle of the fruit fly. Then he tried to concentrate on what Ben Franklin did with that kite. But he couldn't get his mind off Florida. He had an all new worry.

I might miss Mom and Dad a lot—even if they totally ruined my life by moving up here.

CLANG!

The recess bell startled Davy. He nearly fell off his chair. Everyone headed for the door.

"Davy Gonzalez," Mrs. Porter said, "I'd like to talk to you for a minute."

"Uh oh!" Davy muttered. "She's going to ask me about that kite."

But Mrs. Porter had something else on her mind. "Davy," she said, "going to a new school is rough at first. But I think you'll get to like it here. I hope you'll tell me if I can help in any way."

Davy sighed with relief, thanked Mrs. Porter, and hurried out of the room. His red jacket with the yellow stripes on the sleeves was hanging all by itself in the hallway. He put it on and jogged outside.

Davy paced nonstop around the playground. He was worrying about his parents and trying to stay warm. Three snowflakes drifted down from the gray sky. When the bell to end recess clanged, Davy hurried back into the building. Suddenly he had a brainstorm.

Mom and Dad will miss me. They'll miss me so much that they'll move back to Florida! I bet they won't last a week here!

With that problem solved, Davy happily reached into his jacket pocket. He yanked his hand out, gasping. *What was that?* Something furry and bony. Definitely not his letter. Gritting his teeth and holding his breath, he pulled out whatever it was.

A ratty old rabbit's foot. *A rabbit's foot?* Davy plunged his hand back into his pocket. It was empty. He tried the right-hand pocket. His fingers closed around something truly gross—something slimy and sticky. Slowly he pulled it out of his pocket. *YUCK.* A piece of rotten banana peel. Davy noticed something else. His jacket smelled like . . . mustard. Then he realized that this jacket wasn't his.

Davy's heart began to pound. *Where's my . . . ?*

What questions would you want to ask about the things in this jacket?

"Time for reading groups," Mrs. Porter said in a cheery voice. She took the red-and-yellow jacket, hung it on a peg, and shooed Davy into the classroom.

Suzy Vickers read aloud, but Davy didn't even try to listen. He had to get his jacket back. Suppose someone found his letter. Suppose someone read it!

The idea made Davy's hands sweat. He wondered what it was like to die of embarrassment. He began to wish he were a fruit fly.

I've got to calm down, he told himself. *I've got to find my own jacket. I've got to search the hallway.*

He walked up to Mrs. Porter and said, "I've got to go to the bathroom."

She nodded, and Davy rushed out of the room. He grabbed the jacket that wasn't his and headed straight for the far end of the hallway. Taking a deep breath, he started marching past the long line of jackets and coats hanging on pegs. His eyes checked out each garment.

Green. Purple. Black. Orange. Plaid. Tweed. Checked. Dotted. No. No. No. No . . . Yes! There it was! Another red-and-yellow jacket—at the corner where the hallway turned right. Davy reached for it and pulled. Something, or someone, pulled back.

It was a boy with floppy red hair and approximately ten thousand freckles. Davy knew who he was—Marty Lobel from the other fourth-grade class.

"I think our jackets got switched," Davy said. He thrust the one he was holding toward Marty. "This must be yours."

Marty grabbed the jacket, jammed his hand into the left-hand pocket, and pulled out the rabbit's foot. With a gigantic sigh of relief, he leaned against the wall. "I thought I'd lost it. The greatest good luck charm in the Western Hemisphere."

Davy nodded. "I know what you mean. I thought I'd lost something really important, too." He took the other red-and-yellow jacket off the peg and reached into its left-hand pocket.

"Ugh-h-h!"

Davy's face turned white. He groaned as he pulled his hand out of the pocket. On his palm lay something the size of a thumb, but wrapped in very dirty, very fuzzy, gray wool.

Marty's eyes opened wide. "That's your good luck charm?"

Davy groaned again. "I don't know what it is, but it's not mine."

"Wow, you mean that's someone else's jacket?" Marty asked.

Davy nodded as he dropped the wooly thing back into the pocket. Across the hall, a door opened.

"Marty?"

"That's my teacher!" Marty whispered. Still holding his jacket, he dashed toward the door. "Meet me at lunch," he called over his shoulder. "I'll help you find your jacket."

Davy sprinted back to his own classroom. When the lunch bell finally rang, he made a beeline for the door. Grabbing the second red-and-yellow jacket that wasn't his, he ran to the lunchroom. Marty was waiting for him outside the door.

"Here's my plan," Marty whispered. "We walk past every table in the lunchroom.

We look for the jacket, but we act real casual. Like we're just walking for the fun of it. That way, nobody hassles us."

Davy nodded. He yanked the heavy door open and lunged inside.

CRACK! Davy smashed his head against something hard. Actually it was someone else's head. He winced and rubbed his forehead with both hands. When he looked up, he saw a girl rubbing her forehead. It was Franny MacPhee, a classmate. She was wearing a red-and-yellow jacket.

"I think this is yours," Davy said. He held out the gray wooly thing.

"My giant silkworm moth cocoon!" Franny exclaimed. "I thought I'd lost it."

"A cocoon?" Marty asked as Davy and Franny exchanged jackets. "Cool."

Davy reached into his pocket. He found his letter. Unopened.

By the time the three fourth graders paid for their tuna sandwiches, Franny had explained how caterpillars spin cocoons. By the time they found three seats together, Marty had related the history of his rabbit's foot. By the time they finished eating, Davy had described life in Florida.

A fifth grader stopped to stare at them. "What's this—some kind of club?" He pointed to their three identical jackets.

Franny nodded. "That's exactly right."

Davy turned to Marty. "So what's the banana peel for?"

Marty shrugged. "Oh, that. It's gotten so gross I don't know how to get rid of it. I just keep my hand out of that pocket. And what about that important thing you lost? What is it?"

Davy shrugged. "Oh, just a letter. But I don't really need it after all." ●

What kinds of questions would you like to ask the author of this story?

Before You Read

Think back to two of the questions you had at the beginning of the story. Were you able to answer the questions after reading? If so, how? Were the answers in the story? Did you figure them out from what you already knew? Or are there really no definite answers to your questions? Discuss with a partner.

What If?

What if Davy *had* mailed his letter? Write an answer he might have received from his aunt and uncle.

Pick a Pocket

Get together with a friend and compare notes about what you have in your pockets. (If you don't have a pocket, or your pockets are empty, compare what you have in your backpacks.) Then think about things you've kept in your pockets in the past. What is the grossest thing? The most valuable? The most interesting? Write or draw to show your answers.

Get Organized!

Do things seem to get lost in your bedroom? Maybe you just need to get organized. Check these tips out.

1 The Right Stuff

It's hard to be organized without the right tools. Here are some things that help:

- bulletin board
- wastebasket
- baskets and boxes
- shelves

2 Treasures

Display a favorite collection:

- Make a collage of trading cards on the back of a door.
- Keep small stuffed animals in an over-the-door shoe holder.
- Attach barrettes to a long ribbon. Hang the ribbon on a doorknob.
- Ask permission to string clothesline on one wall. Use clothespins to show off baseball caps.

3 In Plain Sight

Keep things you use most where you can find them:

- Use see-through containers for small items.
- Label storage boxes to tell what's inside and stack them.
- Put a hook on the back of your door for your jacket or robe.
- Keep everything you need for school in one place.

4 Out of Sight

Put away the things you don't need or use often:

- Keep out-of-season clothes at the back of your closet.
- Use under-the-bed boxes for toys you want, but don't play with.
- Give away things you don't want.

Before...

and After!

PET DETECTIVES
by Lisa Rao

IMAGINE THIS:

Your pet poodle is missing. You call Kat Albrecht and tell her your problem. "Don't worry," Kat tells you. "I'll put my two best detectives, AJ and Rachel, on the case. You'll have your poodle back in no time." Great, you think. But there's one more piece of news, and it might surprise you— Kat's two best detectives both have four legs and a tail. They're her dogs!

AJ is a bloodhound and Rachel is a weimaraner. They're both SAR dogs, which stands for "search and rescue." There are hundreds of SAR dogs around the globe that help find missing people. But AJ and Rachel are the very first "pet search-and-rescue" team in the world. Kat is their owner and a retired police officer. AJ and Rachel are retired police canine unit dogs.

Kat knows first-hand how upsetting it is to lose a pet. Four years ago, AJ disappeared. Kat was frantic. She called a friend and coworker who worked with a dog trained in *scent discrimination* (the ability to tell different odors from one another). The dog's name was Thalie.

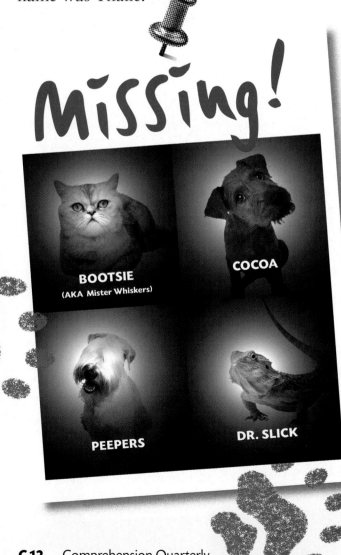

Missing!

BOOTSIE
(AKA Mister Whiskers)

COCOA

PEEPERS

DR. SLICK

Kat gave Thalie the blanket AJ slept on, hoping she could sniff it and pick up AJ's scent. Within 15 minutes, Thalie tracked down AJ in the neighborhood, not far from home. This made Kat realize that the same talents SAR dogs use to find people could be transferred to track down other pets as well. She started training AJ and Rachel to do the job.

HOT ON THE TRAIL

In the past three years, AJ and Rachel have located 18 missing cats and 10 dogs. But they've found other types of missing pets as well. They've found missing snakes, iguanas, a ferret, a gecko, and even a horse! "AJ's better at finding other dogs," Kat told us. "But for some reason, Rachel just loves to search for lost kitties."

We asked Kat if there were any other differences in AJ and Rachel. "I would say Rachel is more of a 'people person,'" Kat said. "While they're both very affectionate dogs, Rachel's personality is much more bubbly and friendly. Her tail is constantly wagging, and she loves meeting new people. AJ is calmer. He's not unfriendly—just more reserved." Kat also says that AJ sometimes seems to be more in his own world. "Rachel always comes to me immediately if I call her," Kat said. "Sometimes with AJ, it takes a few tries."

We asked Kat if her two pet detectives ever seem to get frustrated or upset. "The only time they seem to get

What questions would you ask Kat about her two dogs?

frustrated is if it's dinnertime and their food isn't ready," Kat said with a laugh. "And you can't blame them for that. I feel that way when my dinner's late, too!"

THE NOSE KNOWS

SAR dogs are trained to find people by using their amazing sense of smell. Try these two experiments: Gather a bunch of colored pencils in as many colors as you can find, and in as many shades as possible. Show them to two friends and ask them to pick out a red one. Now ask them to pick out another red pencil, a shade darker. This is easy for humans, unless we're color blind. It's as simple as breathing, because we have the ability to see different shades of color easily. But a dog cannot do this.

Now take 20 identical pencils and put them on a table. Have your friends turn around or close their eyes so they cannot see what you do next. Rub your hands on only one pencil and put it back on the table. Ask your friends to smell all the pencils and tell you which one you rubbed with your hands. Tell them you'll give them a thousand dollars each if they get it right the first time! Not only will they think you're crazy, but even if they believed the part about the money, they simply couldn't do it. There's no way humans could ever use their sense of smell that way. But an SAR dog can.

SAR dogs can't tell the difference between shades of color—not for all the doggie treats in the world! But on the other hand, you can ask them to follow a track in

Rachel

Kat Albrecht gives Detective Rachel the scent of a missing cat. Police officers do the same thing when they want police bloodhounds to find missing people.

tall grass and they can do it. You can ask them to pick out pebbles that look exactly like all the other pebbles, but differ only in that they've been touched by a particular person, and they can do it. They can locate an object that in every way is physically identical to other objects near it, except for having been touched by its handler. Good SAR dogs can do this again and again, and all they want is a pat on the head for their reward.

Some SAR dogs can locate money that has been touched by people who were handling drugs, and at the same time, may even locate small amounts of drugs that have been wrapped, sealed, and hidden within layers of other material. Other SAR dogs are able to locate a lost child buried under a snowdrift, where sight and sound are useless. They can do this all with their sense of smell—the amazing gift with which SAR dogs have been blessed.

If there's a missing pet to be found, AJ and Rachel can find it. "It's just a matter of giving them something with the lost pet's scent on it," Kat says. "Then it's really only a matter of time. Give them a scent on a sweater, a blanket, a food dish—that's all they'll need. I say the magic words, *take scent,* and they're off."

What more would you like to know about SAR dogs?

WRONG PET!

Are AJ and Rachel ever wrong? "It's very rare, but it happens," Kat says. "One day Rachel and I were out searching for a missing cat. When Rachel finds the scent she's looking for, she becomes very excited. Her entire body starts wiggling, not just her tail.

"Suddenly, Rachel became very excited. Her entire body was twitching and her tail was wagging like crazy. 'Good girl,' I told her, thinking she's found our missing kitty. Well, what she found was fluffy, had four legs, and a tail. But it wasn't a cat *or* a dog. It was a *skunk!*"

found!

Detective Rachel has used her keen sense of smell to help locate more than 14 missing cats and at least one skunk!

WHAT'S NEXT?

But what happens when AJ and Rachel get too old to search? "Sadly, I don't think Rachel and AJ will do too much more searching," Kat told us. "Rachel has some heart problems, and AJ has problems with his hip. Dogs need to retire from their jobs when they get too old, just like people."

Are there any pet detective dogs in training? "You bet there are! AJ is already helping me train some new bloodhounds for when he retires," Kat said. "I already have a new bloodhound named Chase, who shows a lot of promise. And we're hoping to begin training a brand new team of pet rescue dogs very soon."

Kat is very excited that police forces and scientists are just now starting to treat a missing pet case with almost the same respect they treat a missing person case. "Not only will we have teams of trained dogs ready to help find missing pets, but the police will be using state-of-the-art equipment as well," Kat explained. "Police units now use infrared cameras to help them find missing pets. And DNA tests that have only been used to identify people are now just starting to be used to identify pets. A DNA match is like a fingerprint—no two are exactly alike. A police squad recently used DNA from cells in a cat whisker to help them find a missing cat! It's very exciting to be part of all this new technology and help people find their missing animals."

We asked Kat what advice she'd give to kids who want to have a job like hers when they grow up. "You'd have to be a very patient person," Kat said. "It takes a lot of work to train a bloodhound to do this. And then once your dog is trained, you have to trust him or her completely. Sometimes it looks as if they're going totally off track, but their nose is leading them the right way. And, of course, you have to be an animal lover and must want to help people. Personally, I think I have the best job in the world!" ○

What questions would you ask Kat about her job?

Shh! Listen...

New tools, like this amplified listening device, help to detect the faint meows of trapped cats and the movements within pipes of other trapped pets.

ANY QUESTIONS?

After reading the article, what do you still want to learn about SAR dogs? List two questions you have. Then record some ideas about where you might find the answers.

AD CAMPAIGN

Any business needs publicity. In 25 words or less, write an advertisement for Kat Albrecht's pet detective business. Add an illustration to your advertisement.

THE SNIFF TEST

Okay—so you *don't* have an especially sensitive nose. You can still use your sense of smell to tell you about your surroundings. Close your eyes for a few minutes. Concentrate on what you can smell—perfume, markers, cleaning solution, and the ripe banana in someone's lunch, for example. Then open your eyes and list the smells you were able to pick up.

Where Could It Be?

by M.C. Hall

I saw it only yesterday
(Or perhaps the day before).
It was sitting in my bedroom
In the middle of the floor.
I know I didn't move it—
I'd remember if I had.
And, boy, if I don't find it
My mom will be SO mad!
She told me when I got it
That it better not get lost;
Especially when she found out
What the thing was gonna cost.
I don't suppose you've seen it
Somewhere 'round the house?

Oops! I hear Mom screaming!
I think she found my mouse!

eeeeek!

As you read the poem, did you ask yourself what was
lost? Were you able to guess the answer? Write your
own poem about something you've lost.

ASKING QUESTIONS

Look What I Found!

Keiko is doing some research about long-ago explorers. She's reading a chart that shows several explorers who ended up someplace other than where they were headed. As she reads the chart, Keiko begins **asking questions.** She decides to write down her questions so she can use them to clarify what she reads later and improve her understanding.

EXPLORER	WHERE HE WAS HEADED...	WHERE HE ENDED UP...
Christopher Columbus	(1492) Headed west from Spain to find India	Landed on the island of San Salvador in North America
John Cabot	(1497) Sailed northwest from England looking for a shorter route to India	Landed in what is now Canada
Ferdinand Magellan	(1519) Left Portugal and sailed southwest to find a route from the Atlantic Ocean to the Pacific Ocean	Sailed up a big river in South America
Henry Hudson	(1609) Left Holland to find a northern route to the Pacific Ocean	Explored what is now known as Hudson Bay in Canada

Keiko's Questions

Why were so many explorers looking for a passage to the Pacific and India?

Did anyone ever find it? Who? When?

What kind of people were these explorers?

What made them want to explore?

Now Keiko can use her questions as she reads about each of the explorers to find the answers and to help understand her reading about the explorers as a group.

SOMETHING'S OUT THERE

by Elizabeth Van Steenwyk

Randi couldn't wait to go canoeing and camping again. She and her folks came to the Missouri River in Montana every year. Now they drove to Coal Bank Landing to begin the trip down the river. Soon her dad turned off the highway onto a dirt road, and Randi saw Uncle Andy's van and her cousin Jessie standing by the loading ramp, waving to her.

Dad parked, and Randi leaped out of the car. She ran up to Jessie and they slapped high fives.

"You ready?" Jessie yelled.

"I've been ready for weeks," Randi yelled back.

"Guess what? We're stopping at the campsites where Lewis and Clark stayed on their 'Voyage of Discovery,'" Jessie said. "Maybe we'll find something they left behind."

"It'll be about 200 years old then," Randi told her.

"What do *you* know about Lewis and Clark?" Jessie asked.

"I just finished reading a book about them." Randi tossed a pebble into the river nearby. "I liked reading about Seaman, Captain Lewis' big, black dog. He was a Newfoundland. That's my favorite breed of dog. He once had a fight with a huge bear."

"He must have been really brave," Jessie replied.

"He sure was!" Randi said. "I wonder what happened to him after the trip ended."

"Who knows?" Jessie answered. "Let's go."

Randi helped her mom and dad load all their stuff into a canoe. Then they shoved off downstream. Randi sat in the bow, her mom in the center, and her dad at the stern. The rhythm of paddling a canoe returned easily to Randi, and soon she pulled with the current.

"Lookin' good," Jessie called from her canoe as she rowed past with Uncle Andy and Aunt Sue.

Randi sighed as she looked around. The scenery was awesome. Sometimes she felt that nothing was real—it looked like part of an adventure movie. She looked at the tall cliffs and the canyons in between. She wondered where they went.

She stared and stared. What was that? Did something move along those rocky walls? It looked kind of black—furry too, and fast. It was keeping up with their canoe.

Randi glanced around. Had anyone else seen it? She'd ask Jessie as soon as she could.

A rain squall hit just as they came ashore, and Randi couldn't think of anything else but setting up shelter. She jumped into a tent with her folks and dried off with a towel. She loved hearing the sound of rain pattering on the tent. But she couldn't get that black, furry thing out of her mind.

"We'll start the campfire as soon as the rain stops," her dad said. "Hamburgers tonight."

"Good." Randi looked around for the snack bag. "I'm starving." She grabbed a box of raisins. "When will we get to Hole in the Wall?" she asked. Maybe if that black animal was still following them, she could look for tracks. What if it was a bear, though? What would she do?

What questions do you have about the story so far?

Randi crawled into her
sleeping bag right after supper and
slept soundly until daylight. Suddenly,
she was wide awake. What was that noise?
It sounded like a whine.

She peeked outside. Something dark
scampered through the cottonwood trees just
beyond the campsite. She started to unzip the tent.

"Randi."

She whirled around. "Dad! Sorry if I woke you."

"You shouldn't wander off," her dad warned. "It's easy to get
lost out here."

"Right." Randi sighed as she looked toward the trees. Whatever
was following them wanted something. Food, maybe? No, there was
food around. Was it lonesome? Then why didn't it come nearer?

The group put their canoes into the river after breakfast with plans
to stop at the Hole for lunch. Randi watched carefully as she paddled,
hoping to see the black animal. But she saw nothing. She felt disappointed.

At noon they pulled into shore near the Hole in the Wall.

"Race you to the top," Jessie called.

Randi looked up at the cliff with the big hole in it. "You're on!"

"Be careful," Mom called.

Randi and Jessie started out. As they went, Randi told her cousin
about what she had seen. As they debated about what it could have
been, Randi heard a rustling noise in the bushes. They stopped. An
animal suddenly appeared out of nowhere. It was a dog—a big, black
dog, and he was holding a stick in his mouth!

"Hey, are you lost?" Jessie asked and stepped toward him. The dog
stepped back into the bushes, leaving the stick.

"Wait!" Randi called. "Don't go." She grabbed the stick, followed
the dog, and saw its tail disappearing around a rock. The girls ran to
keep up. The dog waited, then ran forward, waited, then ran some more.

"He's playing a game," Randi said. "He's teasing us." She threw the stick and the dog grabbed it. The girls and the dog chased each other and ran around, over and over again, without stopping. Suddenly the dog dropped the stick, then threw himself on the ground, just out of reach, and lay there panting. The girls threw themselves on the ground, too, out of breath and sweating.

Randi wondered how long they'd been playing. She stared at the dog as she caught her breath. He looked so much like a Newfoundland. His bigness, his turned-up nose, his thick fur . . . Randi sat up straight.

"You *are* a Newfie," she cried, "just like . . ." She stared hard. She looked at Jessie and then back at the dog. She felt so strange. She blinked hard.

"I know who you are," she said softly. "You're . . . you're . . ."

"Randi! Jessie!" Randi's dad burst through the tall grass. "Are you two all right?"

"We were worried when you were gone so long." Randi's mom quickly caught up, followed by Jessie's parents.

What questions would you ask Randi and Jessie about the dog they saw?

"We're okay," Randi said. "We started following that dog and sort of forgot the time."

Their parents looked around. "What dog?" they asked.

Randi looked in the shade of a cottonwood. "Over there," she said. But she couldn't see anything. "He was right there."

"He was! It's true!" Jessie added.

"Let's go, you two." Jessie's dad helped them to their feet.

Everyone started down the trail. Randi hurried over to the place where she had tossed the stick to the dog. The stick was right there, on the ground.

"Wait for us," Randi whispered. "We'll finish the game when we come back next year!" ⚪

WHY ASK WHY?

List two or three questions you had as you read this story. Were you able to find the answers in the story or will you need to do some research? You may want to look in a dog book to find out what a Newfoundland looks like, or you may have to imagine the answer to, "Why weren't Randi and Jessie scared of the dog?"

REAL—OR NOT?

What do you think about Randi's story?
Did she really see the dog? Or was it a dream?
Fold a sheet of paper in half. On the top half, list your ideas about why you think the dog was real. On the bottom half, list your ideas about why you think it wasn't.

LOST POEMS

Have you ever been lost—even for just a little while? How did you feel? Write a short poem, rhymed or unrhymed, about the experience or the feeling of being lost. Add a drawing to your poem.

Ancient Egypt Uncovered

by Carol Hosking

2,000 years ago a busy city lay at the mouth of a wide river that emptied into a beautiful blue sea. The people of this city traveled by boat up and down the river and across the sea and became the biggest traders in the region. Soon they were among the richest, as well. People from other countries came to admire the city's splendid palaces, gardens, and temples. But then the city disappeared off the face of the earth. What happened to it has been a mystery for hundreds of years . . . until now.

This Egyptian city was called Herakleion, and it stood at the mouth of the Nile River on the edge of the Mediterranean Sea for 1,000 years

or more. But some time almost 1,300 years ago, it mysteriously disappeared.

Then, in June 2000, after many months of searching, archaeologists had enough evidence to announce that they had located the whole city. French underwater archaeologist Franck Goddio announced the discovery of Herakleion. "We have an entire city, frozen in time," he told news reporters. He and his team were ready to show their work to the world. About four miles from the shore, under the waters of the Mediterranean Sea, divers had discovered the underwater buildings of Herakleion.

Time had stood still since the city had disappeared. The city lay untouched—

pottery lay undisturbed near the city's walls, but coins and jewelry were scattered in the streets. Had people dropped these as they ran? What had they been running from?

Scientists around the world called the find "the most exciting discovery in the history of underwater archaeology." To be sure, there is plenty of other buried treasure in the Mediterranean Sea, but the lost city of Herakleion had been high on scientists' most-wanted list. Why?

Why was Herakleion important?

Long ago, sea traders sailing the Mediterranean Sea made Herakleion a busy place. It was located on two major water routes—a branch of the Nile River and the Mediterranean Sea. Barges and ships regularly passed through its ports in both directions. The rich soil at the river mouth near Herakleion helped the people grow plenty of food that they could trade for goods from other countries. Skilled workers within the city made fabric, jewelry, rope, baskets, perfume, and glass to sell.

Some of these goods were sent upriver, and others were sent by sea throughout the Mediterranean world. In exchange, things such as horses, wood, ivory, and spices were brought into the city.

Herakleion grew, and its citizens became wealthy.

What would you want to know about life back then?

About the same time, however, Alexander the Great built an even grander city nearby. His city, Alexandria, became the capital city of Egypt at the time. But Herakleion remained an important place.

Ancient Greeks traveled to the shores of Egypt and described the area's riches and arts in their writing. They wrote about Herakleion's magnificent mansions and gardens. They observed amazing banquets, sporting games, and contests.

Top: Head of white marble sculpture lies on sea floor.
Bottom: Dates and images on gold coins help scientists discover more about Herakleion.

How did archaeologists know where to look?

As with most explorations, the first "digging" began in a library! The archaeologists first researched all they could about Herakleion. They read what the ancient Greeks had written about the city. They studied other writings and historical maps of the area. They found out a lot about Herakleion before they actually began to dig.

Scientific records also showed that large parts of the Egyptian coast had vanished during a series of earthquakes, fires, and floods. Many people were afraid that the treasures of Herakleion were lost forever at the bottom of the sea.

Scientists explore the seabed in a special submarine that uses high-tech equipment.

How did archaeologists find the buried city?

You might wonder why it took so long to find this buried city. After all, the remains of Herakleion are only 4 miles offshore and 30 feet deep! But it hasn't been as easy as it might sound. The city was not only underwater, but also buried under many layers of sand and dirt on the seafloor.

Divers have had to work through the muddy water and weeds clogging the shore to even reach bottom. That's when the real searching began. Slowly and carefully, the divers have sifted the salty sands that covered the city. It's been difficult work, and even after a few years' time, the work continues.

Mr. Goddio leads the project, but it is very much a team effort. The work is expensive and requires the support of several organizations. Professional divers, archaeologists, historians, and scientists must all work together to locate the remains and interpret their findings.

The scientists rely on many kinds of high-tech equipment for their answers. A *magnetometer* finds the exact location of metal objects, even if they are buried in the deep sand and mud.

Sonar helps determine how big and how deep each thing is by sending out soundwaves. These soundwaves "bounce" when they meet an object. The scientists use the soundwaves to make a map that shows where each piece of the buried city is at the bottom of the sea.

Franck Goddio's research boat may look simple, but it has lots of special equipment on board.

Echo sounders are used to find out how deep the water is. This helps the team make a map of the seafloor.

Divers explore the ocean with high-tech submarines, including remote-controlled cameras and underwater vehicles. They make videotapes and send other information to the laboratories on shore and in the research boat.

Back on land, many people are piecing together what happened to Herakleion—and when. Scientists think that the city suffered an earthquake because the walls of the city are all leaning in the same direction on the seafloor. Historians have studied the dates on coins and jewelry and think that the earthquake happened about 1,300 years ago.

Think of at least two questions you would ask the divers and scientists.

What has happened to the treasure brought up by the divers?

So far, only a few pieces of the buried treasure have been brought up out of the water. Even though the pieces aren't down too deep, it is a big job. Large pieces have to be bolted securely into a steel frame. Then they are carefully attached to the deck of the research boat. Even with special handling, there is always the danger that some of the pieces might break or fall onto the ones still below.

What has been brought to land has to be treated to remove layers of salt. When the scientists are finished with them, some of the pieces will be sent to museums.

However, many people, called *preservationists*, would like to leave most of Herakleion where it is. Franck Goddio agrees. He suggested they open an underwater museum, possibly with glass-walled viewing tunnels. Then visitors would be able to see the treasures where they fell.

Meanwhile, there is still a lot to be learned about Herakleion. The work of the scientists and historians is only beginning. In the years to come, we can expect to see models of Herakleion that will show what its buildings and gardens probably looked like. We will be able to look with wonder on the same marvels of art and architecture that delighted ancient rulers and ordinary citizens.

Best of all, of course, would be the real thing—to glide back in time through the streets of ancient Herakleion itself. Maybe someday you'll be able to cruise on a glass-bottomed boat over an amazing underwater museum. ◉

Buried Treasure

Everyday things tell people about life in the past. These things might be considered treasure someday. Think about things that are important to you. List five items that might survive to tell someone far in the future about *your* life.

In The News

Write a short news story about the discovery of Herakleion. Be sure your story answers the following questions: Who? What? Where? When? and Why?

Watery Museum

Imagine that you are asked to design an underwater museum. List or draw several exhibits your museum might feature.

Finding the Past

Lost cities like Herakleion help us find out about the past. What are some questions you have about Ancient Egypt that you might research? What are two things you think Herakleion's buried treasures can teach us?

Lost-and-Found Ad

Imagine that you have lost a pet or something else you care about. Write an ad for the lost-and-found section of the newspaper. Describe your missing pet or item and explain how someone who finds it can get in touch with you. Ask yourself questions to be sure your ad includes all the necessary information.

Discovery!

Have you ever found a four-leaf clover? a dollar bill? a fossil? What's the most exciting or interesting thing you've found? Write a short story about your favorite discovery.

Songwriting

Choose a familiar tune and make up new words to create a song about making a discovery, getting lost, or losing something.

Tune: "I've Been Workin' on the Railroad"

I've been looking for my backpack,
Everywhere I go.
It's been gone for seven weeks now,
And I miss it so.

More Books

Erickson, John R. *Lost in the Dark Uncharted Forest*. Puffin, 1999.

Gerstein, Mordecai. *Behind the Couch*. Hyperion, 1996.

Patent, Dorothy Hinshaw. *Lost City of Pompeii*. Benchmark, 2000.

Reid, Struan. *The Children's Atlas of Lost Treasures*. Millbrook, 1997.

Tokuda, Wendy and Richard Hall. *Humphrey, the Lost Whale: A True Story*. Heian, 1992.

On the Web

The Search for New Species
http://animal.discovery.com/quest/
quest.html

Shipwreck Treasure Hunting Photos
http://www.ellawarley.com/
Photo8UW.html

Great Finds
http://www.pbs.org/wgbh/pages/
roadshow/stories/index.html

Search Dog
http://www.nmbe.unibe.ch/abtwt/
saint_bernard.html

Across the Curriculum

Research
Do some research to find out about one of the lost "treasures" listed below or choose a topic of your own. Share what you learn in the form of a poster, short report, or videotaped "news report."
- Wreck of the Titanic
- City of Pompeii
- King Tut's Tomb
- El Dorado

Debate
Stage a classroom debate. Have two teams, each of which researches and debates in favor of one of the following points of view:
- Objects from past civilizations should be put in museums/should be left where they are found. **– or –**
- Lost items belong to the person who found them/to the person who lost them.

Have YOU Seen MY...?

Although they use few words, oh—the stories ads can tell. Just take a look at this newspaper's Lost and Found section. What do the ads say to you? What do they make you wonder about?

LOST DOG

Miniature poodle named Hercules. Red collar and a red-and-white striped doggie sweater. Reward for safe return. 555-2736.

HELP!

Lost iguana. 24 inches long, including tail. Missing since Friday. Last seen in my car in South Mall parking lot. Call 555-6810.

MISSING

Diary. VERY PRIVATE. If found, DO NOT read. Plaid cover. Lost in Branson Park. Call 555-6799. Desperate!

CAT FOUND

Cute black kitten with one blue eye, one green. Female. Collar says "Abby." Claim by calling 555-0023.

FOUND!

Eyeglasses. Rhinestone-studded with pink lenses. Left at the Park Street bus stop. Call 555-9833.

IS IT YOURS?

Huge, hungry lizard. Found yesterday at South Mall Candy Shoppe. Call 555-2874 soon!

REWARD!

$50 reward for return of female cat. Yellow striped fur; green eyes. Collar says "Muffy." Phone 555-8364, after 5 P.M.

FOUND

Plaid diary. Claim by telling what happened on January 8. Wow! Call 555-1796. Reward expected.

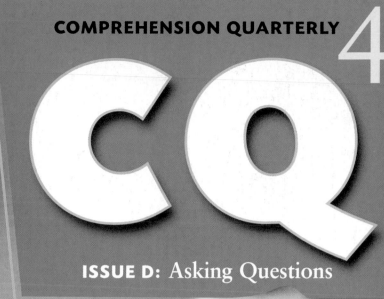

COMPREHENSION QUARTERLY

CQ

4

ISSUE D: Asking Questions

PROD.

Behind the Scenes

SLATE	TAKE
4.8D	1

DATE

Behind the Scenes

THINK ABOUT: Asking Questions

D4

FICTION
Nikash's Sugar Sculptures
Nikash's move was hard until he found a way to bring something special from his old home to his new one.

D11

NONFICTION
Special Effects, Specially Done
Find out what makes the movies you enjoy so exciting, magical, and scary!

D19

FICTION
In the Land of the Ticos
Join Paula as she explores Costa Rican rain forests with her favorite relatives.

D24

NONFICTION
All Fired Up!
Meet some of the authors who wrote the stories and articles for these magazines. Find out why they like to write just for YOU!

ASKING QUESTIONS

It's Magic!

Tyrell is an amateur magician who is always looking for magic tricks to amaze his friends. That's why he has his nose buried in *Easy Magic Tricks.*

This one looks interesting, Tyrell thinks as he finds a trick called "Mind Power."

Tyrell knows that **asking questions** as he reads is a good way to check whether or not he understands what to do. For every genre, or type of writing, the questions Tyrell asks will be different. For how-to directions, such as magic tricks, Tyrell knows that it's important to understand and follow every step exactly. Notice the types of questions Tyrell asks as he reads about "Mind Power."

Mind Power

Hmmm. The directions are in two parts. I wonder why? Oh, I get it. The first part tells how to do the trick. The second part tells how the magician does it.

I wonder if the magician is really concentrating, or if that is part of the trick?

The Trick: The magician tells the audience that he will demonstrate mind reading. The magician asks for a volunteer to touch something in the room after he leaves. After the magician returns, he asks for a different volunteer to point at objects until he identifies the correct one. The magician concentrates carefully as the volunteer points. Suddenly, the magician says "Stop!" To everyone's amazement, he has identified the correct object.

Wow! How does the magician do it?

How It's Done: The second volunteer is your accomplice. This person has a signal to tell you which object was chosen. Just before your accomplice points to the chosen object, he or she will point to a black object.

Oh, is an accomplice someone who's in on the trick?

Think about a time you asked questions as you read. What kinds of questions did you ask? How did your questions help you better understand the genre and the meaning of the text?

NIKASH'S SUGAR SCULPTURES

by Jyotsna Sreenivasan

"You mean we're not going to celebrate Sankranti this year?" Nikash stared at his mother in disbelief. They were standing in the kitchen—their new American kitchen, in their new American apartment—and Nikash was loading the dishwasher as Amma rinsed the dishes. This was one thing his mother didn't like about living in the United States. They had been living in Virginia for six months now, but still his mother missed having a servant, like the one she had in India, to do the dishes and wash the clothes.

"Nikash, I don't have time to celebrate every little holiday!" Amma wiped a strand of hair from her face with her wet hand. Nikash's mother and father were both computer engineers and were very busy all week long.

"But Sankranti isn't a little holiday!" Nikash protested. He remembered celebrating the harvest festival every January when they had lived in India. All their neighbors and relatives had given each other little packets of *ellu*. It was made of sesame seeds, dried coconut chunks, roasted peanuts, tiny chickpeas, and brown sugar cubes. And every year his grandmother, Ajji, made "sugar sculptures" by pouring sugar syrup into molds. Nikash especially loved the sugar sculptures of animals—elephants, monkeys, or turtles. Ajji also made sculptures of bananas, coconuts, and other fruits. "Everyone celebrates Sankranti!" Nikash insisted. "Everyone gives out ellu!"

> The author uses many Indian words in the story. How have you figured out what each one means?

"Only in our state in India," his father said, bringing more dirty dishes from the dining room. "It's only done in Karnataka. Not very many Indians here in Virginia give out ellu."

"Well, we could show them how!" Nikash suggested. "Can you make the ellu tomorrow, Amma? I can even give some to my friends at school on Friday!"

"Nikash, I don't have time to go to the Indian grocery store and pick up all the ingredients," Amma said as she hand-soaped a wooden spoon. "Anyway, it doesn't look much like harvest time here, does it?" She pointed out the window, through which Nikash could see leafless trees and a dusting of snow on the rooftops.

At first Nikash had loved the cold weather. But now he was tired of it. He felt homesick for India—for warm days with bright flowers blooming everywhere, delicious fruits like mangoes and guavas to eat, and his grandmother frying spicy snacks in the kitchen. And he really wanted to celebrate Sankranti.

The doorbell rang, and his father went to answer it. His friend Ryan walked in and said, "Hi, Nikash. Are you ready to do homework?"

Nikash sighed. "I guess so." They spread their books out on the dining room table. Nikash tried to concentrate on his homework, but he kept thinking of Sankranti. Nikash was working on some math problems when he suddenly had an idea about how they could celebrate Sankranti after all. He was so excited, he could hardly concentrate on his homework. "Can you come over to my house after school tomorrow?" he whispered to Ryan.

The next day after school, Nikash opened his dresser drawer and took out the envelope of money his parents had given him for New Year's Day.

"What are we going to do?" Ryan asked.

"You'll see," Nikash said.

He asked Debbie, the young woman who stayed with him until his parents came home, to drive them to the grocery store down the street. "We're going to get all the ingredients we need to celebrate an Indian holiday," he told Ryan. He couldn't wait for his parents to get home. They would be so surprised!

But as soon as they stepped into the grocery story, Nikash froze. The American store was huge! In India, the stores were small, and he knew where everything was. Some stores were so small that he just asked the man at the counter for everything he wanted. But here, he knew he would never be able to find what he needed.

"What's wrong, Nik?" Ryan asked.

"I . . . I think I should go home," Nikash whispered. "I . . . my parents will be home soon." He was too embarrassed to admit to Ryan that he didn't know where to find anything in this giant store.

"But what about the Indian holiday?" Ryan asked.

Nikash swallowed nervously. He really *did* want to celebrate Sankranti, but how could he ever find the things he needed? Then he had an idea. "Ryan, we need to find things fast. Will you help me?"

"Sure," said Ryan.

Nikash sighed with relief. He was surprised at how easy it was to ask for help! He told Ryan what he needed for ellu, and Ryan expertly guided him from one aisle to another. They couldn't find brown sugar cubes, so they bought powdered brown sugar, and they couldn't find dried coconut pieces, so they got shredded coconut. They had to forget about the chickpeas—Ryan didn't even know what they were!

"Are we going to make cookies?" Ryan asked.

Nikash shook his head. What he really wanted to make were sugar sculptures. He knew he could never find the sculpture molds in the United States, and even if he did, he wouldn't know how to make the sculptures. Ajji always knew the exact moment when the syrup was just right and ready to be poured into the molds.

"I need some kind of candy," Nikash said. "Candy that's shaped like different things—like animals, or fruits."

"Here are some candy bears," Ryan said. "And some candy lizards."

Nikash frowned. "No," he said. "They have to be beautiful."

"Does it have to be candy?" Ryan asked.

"Well, it should be sweet, at least," Nikash said.

Ryan said, "I have an idea!" He took Nikash to a different section of the store and showed him little tubes that looked like toothpaste, and little packets of what looked like silver and gold beads.

"What do you do with these?" Nikash asked.

Now it was Ryan's turn to be mysterious. "You'll see. My mother uses these all the time." He also picked up some plain sugar cookies.

Nikash was already at work in the kitchen with Ryan when his parents came home. He and Ryan had been squeezing icing onto the cookies, and decorating them with the silver and gold beads, which Nikash discovered were actually little candies! Nikash had decorated his cookies with mangoes and flowers. Ryan had drawn baseballs and footballs on his.

"Look!" Nikash cried as he showed his mother the bowl full of sesame seeds, shredded coconut, and brown sugar. "I made ellu! But it doesn't look like Indian ellu."

His father filled a spoon with the ellu and ate it. "It's delicious!" he said.

"And we're decorating these cookies," Nikash added. "They don't look like sugar sculptures, but at least they are beautiful and sweet."

"What a great idea!" Amma said as she looked

How does Nikash and Ryan's dialogue help you better understand the harvest festival?

at the tubes of icing and candy beads. "I wonder if we can ship some of these to India? Our friends and relatives there would love these."

"Nikash, we have a surprise for you, too," his father said as he held out a brown cardboard box. "Ajji sent this for you."

Nikash opened the box, and there before his eyes were three perfect sugar sculptures—an elephant, a turtle, and a monkey! He picked up one of the pure white sculptures and held it in his palm—but not for too long. He was afraid it might melt and make his hand sticky. There was also a bag of real Indian ellu!

Ryan tasted some of the Indian ellu. "Why do you give out sesame seeds during this festival?" he asked.

"The sesame seeds represent the seeds the farmers gather at the harvest," Amma explained. "We add the sugar and coconut to make it taste good."

"Now I'll be able to give my friends real ellu!" Nikash exclaimed.

"You should also give them the cookies you and Ryan made, because this is our first American Sankranti," Amma said.

And the next day, that is just what Nikash did. ◐

What questions do you still have about Sankranti?

Celebrating Sankranti

What questions did you have as you read about Sankranti? After you finished reading the story, what else did you want to know about this East Indian harvest festival? Gather information about Sankranti by searching the Internet and reading books and articles. Once you're an "expert" on Sankranti, volunteer to answer your classmates' questions about the festival.

A World of Difference

The states of Karnataka and Virginia are on different continents thousands of miles apart and have very different climates. What are some other differences between Karnataka, where Nikash used to live, and his new home in Virginia? Use a Venn diagram or another graphic organizer to help you list the differences mentioned in the story. Which state would you rather live in? Why?

Holiday Traditions

With a small group of classmates, discuss different holiday traditions. Some of the questions you might ask are: What is your favorite holiday? What special traditions or customs are part of your celebration of this holiday? Why do you think holiday traditions are important?

The Moon Festival

An important holiday celebrated by Chinese communities around the world is the Moon Festival. The Moon Festival is held on the 15th day of the 8th lunar month. It celebrates the biggest and brightest full moon of the year—the harvest moon. The festival, which honors the moon goddess, Chang-O, began in ancient times when Chinese farmers planted and harvested using the Moon as a guide.

During the Moon Festival, families join together to gaze at the Moon, recite moon poems, sing, dance, and worship. Many families have a midnight banquet, and throughout the festival, everyone feasts on moon cakes, round pastries filled with red bean paste and egg yolks or fruits and preserves. The moon cakes are often piled in pyramids of 13 to represent the 13 months of the Chinese year.

Preparations for the Moon Festival begin many weeks before the holiday. The smell of baking moon cakes fills the air. People make colorful paper lanterns to decorate their houses. They set up altars in the corner of a room with dishes of round fruits that symbolize the moon and family togetherness.

Everyone hopes for cloudless skies on the night of the Moon Festival so they can see the harvest moon clearly. The only thing that can ruin the Moon Festival is . . . you guessed it . . . an eclipse of the moon!

SPECIAL EFFECTS, SPECIALLY DONE

BY MIKE GRAF

An alien spacecraft soars toward Earth at an alarming speed. It enters the atmosphere and suddenly . . . nnnnr! nnnnr! . . . laser rays shoot down. In the city below, buildings crumble and fires blaze from the first strikes of the alien weapons. Thousands of people run into the streets in terror. Suddenly, someone points to something streaking across the sky. Everyone cheers, knowing Earth will be saved.

Although the above scene may seem scary and real, it could only happen in a movie, and only with the use of special effects.

Special effects is the art of creating pictures and sounds that seem real on the movie screen. Through the use of special effects, a spaceship can land in California,

a superhero can fly over Chicago, and a battle can be fought on a distant planet.

Sometimes special effects are make-believe images, such as talking dogs, menacing monsters, flying cars, and futuristic cities. At other times, special effects are realistic images, such as tornadoes, dinosaurs, and scenes from faraway countries. Realistic images are used when it is too expensive, dangerous, or difficult to film the actual thing.

Special effects have been used in movies for over a hundred years. Some of the earliest special effects were invented by George Melies. In 1899 this French magician directed a movie called *The Conjurer* and used special effects to make himself disappear. Since then, many types of special effects tricks have been created.

Front projection

Front projection is a type of special effect that creates fake scenery behind an actor. To make it look as if someone is ice-skating in the center of a large city, the city scenery is filmed first. Then the city scene is projected onto a screen. When the actor skates in front of the screen, it looks as if she were ice skating in a city setting.

SPECIAL EFFECTS ARE CREATED

Blue-screen photography

With *blue-screen photography*, another type of special effect, an actor or animal is filmed in front of a blue screen. The image is then separated from the blue color and projected onto a different background. This is like cutting out the shape of an animal or actor from a sheet of paper and pasting it onto different scenery, except the image is moving, and so is the scenery!

What questions do you have about the special effects you've read about so far?

Matte painting

Through *matte painting*, scenery created by an artist is combined with real scenery. If a movie director wants a modern city to have a castle, a film of the city is made. Then an artist hand-paints a picture of a castle on a sheet of clear glass, or creates the matte painting on a computer. Space is left around the painting of the castle to make room for the city. Then the matte painting of the castle is blended into the film of the city, making it look as if the castle were a real part of the scenery.

WITH VARIOUS TECHNIQUES.

Stop-motion photography

Stop-motion photography is another technique used in special effects. It is used to make puppets of animals, humans, or other beings seem alive. Motion picture film is made up of a series of still pictures called *frames*. In stop-motion photography, a puppet is placed in a position and filmed for one frame. The puppet is moved a tiny bit and filmed for another frame, then it is moved again and filmed for the next frame. This is repeated for hundreds of frames that will last just a few seconds in the movie. When the film is finally run through a motion projector at normal speed, the movements on each frame blend together to make it seem as if the puppet were actually moving.

As you read about these special effects, can you think of movies in which they might have been used?

PROPS CAN BE MADE SMALL TO MAKE PEOPLE LOOK HUGE!

Animatronics

Animatronics is a type of special effect that creates robots in the form of monkeys, monsters, and even space creatures. A special effects crew controls a robot's movements through remote control. Because animatronics creatures appear to move like living creatures, they can be filmed right along with the actors.

Miniature models are another type of special effect. Rather than filming a real building or other object, less expensive miniature models are often used. On film, the models look like they are life-size.

To create a scene in which a UFO is flying through space, a miniature model of a spaceship can be floated in a lighted tank filled with cloudy water.

Extra large or small sets and props give the illusion that the actors and actresses are not life-size. *Sets* include houses, cities, or jungles where the acting takes place, and *props* are the objects the actors use, like pencils and chairs. Since actors can't really change size, sets and props can be made extra large to make the people seem tiny, or small to make the people seem huge.

Computer-generated images

Computer-generated images can be used to create almost any imaginable effect in movies—blazing fires, talking dinosaurs, or scenes from other planets. Once the images are created on the computer, they can be changed, moved, copied, and combined with other images for the movie. Computer-generated images can even be used to create an entire movie.

Special effects are often used in movies to create weather conditions and natural disasters. To film a violent storm at sea, actors do not need to go out in a real storm. Instead, they can sit safely in a boat in a large pool or pond. A machine creates crashing waves in the water, fans produce powerful winds, and giant overhead sprinklers send down pounding rain. The scene is filmed in front of a blue screen, which can later be replaced with film of an actual storm. When snowstorms are needed in a movie, snowflakes can be made from plastic flakes, bleached potato flakes, or soapsuds.

The next time you go to a movie, see if you can figure out what special effects were used. Then stay in your seat at the end of the show to watch the movie credits, which list everyone involved in the movie and the work they did. What special effects words like *miniature models*, *blue-screen photography*, and *animatronics* do you recognize? How many different people were involved in creating the special effects that made the movie exciting, magical, or scary? One thing is certain—once you've had a peek "behind the scenes" of movie-making, you'll never look at movies the same way again! ●

What strategies did you use to help you visualize how a special effect is created?

Stop and Respond

QUESTIONS ABOUT SPECIAL EFFECTS

What were some questions you had about special effects after you finished reading the article? Were there any parts of the article that you didn't understand? Write down a few of your questions and then reread the article or do some research to answer them.

FLIP BOOK

The stop-motion photography discussed in "Special Effects, Specially Done" works in the same way flip books do. You flip the pages of these little books with your thumb, and the figures seem to move. Make your own flip book. Be sure to use heavy paper so the pages will flip properly. Draw a figure in the same place on each page, but change it slightly. For example, draw the figure so that its feet change position on each page. Then when the pages are flipped, the figure will seem to run.

LIGHTS, CAMERA, ACTION!

Imagine that you have been asked to make a movie about a story or a book you have recently read. What special effects would you use to make the book come to life? Make a drawing that shows how you would use the special effect, and write a short description that tells about it.

WITH A FACE LIKE THAT ...!

Makeup is an important "behind the scenes" part of all theater, movie, and television productions. Makeup can do amazing things—it can make healthy actors look sick or injured, or young people look very old. Makeup can even make ordinary people look like terrifying monsters.

Why not try your hand at makeup? Try some of these special makeup tricks to turn yourself into a hideous, green-faced monster!

What You'll Need:
- old towel
- special-effects wax (also called nose putty)
- water-based face paint
- 2 or 3 paintbrushes of different sizes
- makeup sponge
- colored hair spray

BEFORE

AFTER

How to Do It:
1. Roll a small piece of wax into a ball and place it over the bridge of your nose. Mold the wax into a big hook shape with your fingers or with a spatula. Smooth the edges of the wax onto the sides of your nose.
2. Now use the wax to make some warts. Put small, round pieces of wax onto your chin or the sides of your nose.
3. Tuck an old towel around your neck. With a damp sponge, put green paint all over your face. Brush a little bit of red paint under your eyes. Use a paintbrush to dab red speckles on your cheeks. Then paint on scraggly black eyebrows.
4. Comb your hair in the wrong direction or tease it to make it stick out. Cover your eyes and spray black, green, or red hair spray on your hair.

Now look in the mirror—if you dare! Through the magic of makeup, you've transformed yourself into a very scary creature. But don't worry—with the help of a little face cream, or soap and water, you'll be your old self in no time!

ASKING QUESTIONS

Exploring with Captain Seagull and His Super Sub

Like most kids, Antonia loves reading the series of books about Captain Seagull and his adventures in his "Super Sub"—a miniature nuclear-powered submarine that manages to get into the most interesting (and tiny!) underwater scrapes. Antonia discovered that **asking questions** before, during, and after she read each of the books helped her understand and enjoy them more.

Antonia is just beginning to read "Captain Seagull and His Super Sub Sail in the Sargasso Sea." As she looks through the book before she begins to read, she has some questions about the special text features.

Is this book like the other "Super Sub" books? It looks like it is. The story is in regular type and the dialogue is in speech balloons. And, interesting facts are in colorful shapes of things found in the sea.

After Antonia flips through the book, she begins reading.

Will I need to read this book as carefully as the other "Super Sub" books? I probably will. Even though the story about Captain Seagull is made up, I know from the other books in the series that the science information is true. So, to understand and enjoy this book, I will have to read everything very carefully.

So, as Antonia digs into this latest "Super Sub" book, she reads not only the story about Captain Seagull in the speech balloons, but also all the interesting facts in the colorful sea shapes. Then she looks closely at the illustrations because she knows they will be filled with information and that she'll learn a lot about the Sargasso Sea in a fun way.

By asking questions before, during, and after she reads these unique informational books, Antonia better understands all the special text features in them and can really enjoy all the fun and interesting information they contain.

In the Land of the Ticos

by Sofia Meza Keane

June 10

Wow! We're going on vacation! When I found out today, I just couldn't wait to call my best friend, Clara, and tell her the exciting news! As soon as she came to the phone, I yelled, "Mom and Dad are taking us to Costa Rica!" Clara was excited for me when she heard the news.

Costa Rica is in Central America. When we get there, we're going to the selva. In Spanish, selva means rain forest. We'll visit Tío Ramon—that's my uncle, and Tía Ana—that's my aunt. We'll also see Sara and Guillermo—they're my primos, or cousins.

June 14

For the last couple of days, I've read a lot about the rain forest. There are so many animals in the selva, like jaguars, white-faced monkeys, armadillos, and red-eyed frogs. But the animal that really caught my attention was the sloth (perezoso), a very slow-moving creature that spends most of its time hanging upside down from trees. A sloth looks green because tiny plants called algae grow in its fur. And, caterpillars like to live in the sloth's fur and feed on the algae. Yuck! It sounds to me like perezosos could use a good shower!

June 20

Yesterday we were so excited about our trip, we were running around the house—up and down the stairs, in and out of all the rooms looking for the things we wanted to bring. And we thought we were ready the night before! But just as we were leaving the house, Dad said, "Wait a minute! My keys, where are they? I had them in my pocket a minute ago!" We all stopped in our tracks for a second, then flew like arrows through the house looking for the keys. Then we heard Dad say, "I found them! They were in my pocket the whole time. Let's go, guys. We're running late!" Phew! I never thought I would be so excited to hear the jingling of keys.

> Do Paula's diary entries make it easier or more difficult for you to visualize the events of the story?

June 21

You'll never guess what happened! After all that rushing around, we missed our flight! I was so disappointed, I almost cried. But after a couple of hours, we got on another flight. Finally, we were on our way to the land of the Ticos! That's what Costa Ricans call themselves. Luis, my four-year-old brother, begged to sit next to the window, and when the plane took off, his eyes were as big as saucers. He said: "Paula, look at the buildings and cars! They look like little ants!"

June 22

We arrived very late and we were all so tired. Our tíos were waiting for us at the gate, and we were so happy to see them. We each gave them a kiss on both cheeks and a big bear hug.

At their house, Tía Ana made us hot chocolate, coffee, and tasty pan dulce (sweet bread). Mom told us that this is traditional Costa Rican hospitality. But before Tía Ana could offer us the pan dulce, Luis already had his hand in it! How embarrassing! But soon we were all laughing and talking and eating, and nobody even remembered Luis' poor manners.

June 24

What an awesome adventure we had today at the Monteverde Cloud Forest! The forest is foggy because it is so high up, and it's hot and humid because it's so near the equator. We saw ferns and leaves as big as Luis and my little prima, Sara. We tried to see who could jump high enough to touch the leaves of the trees and we got pretty sticky and sweaty. Then suddenly, it started to rain. We were soaked before we knew it. Luis was so surprised by the rain, he ran like a jaguar back to the house. Oops! I guess I forgot to tell him that it rains every day here! Luis will have to get used to getting wet if he plans to do anything in Costa Rica!

June 25

We continued to explore the Monteverde Cloud Forest today on a high tram. That's the only way to get to the station at the top of the canopy—the top layer of the rain forest. You could say we had a bird's-eye view of the rain forest because we saw lots of multicolored macaws and toucans. What beautiful birds!

Which animals and land features that Paula describes are unfamiliar to you?

I felt a little lightheaded when I realized how high up I was, but I wouldn't have missed the adventure for anything! With binoculars we spotted two-toed sloths, howler monkeys, and boa constrictors. Luis was so fascinated by the monkeys, he started howling himself. Oh, brother!

June 27

Today was another cool adventure! We went to Manuel Antonio Park. It's on the Pacific Coast. The beach was beautiful. Guillermo and I had fun covering Sara and Luis with the white sand. Then we went snorkeling. At first I was nervous because I had never snorkeled before. But once I was in the water, I felt just like a fish! It was incredible to see all the colorful, exotic fish appearing and disappearing right before my eyes. I took lots of amazing pictures with my waterproof camera.

June 29

We're having so much fun with our tíos! Tío Ramón tells funny knock-knock jokes, and Tía Ana is very thoughtful and caring. She knows we love fruit, so she makes sure there are always many mangoes, papayas, and piñas (pineapples) in her fruit basket. Yesterday my tía bought a sandía—a watermelon—the size of a basketball! It was so sweet and juicy that when I bit into it, it squirted all over my blouse! My tía laughed and said, "¡Lo que tiene de grande lo tiene de jugosa!" Mom said that means "The bigger, the sweeter!"

What questions do you have about the meanings of the Spanish words in Paula's diary?

June 30

Talk about excitement and adventure! Today we took a jerky, jumpy jeep ride to the Arenal Volcano, the most active volcano in Costa Rica. We rode in the back of the jeep, singing songs and screaming every time we went over a bump in the road. But we were speechless when we saw the lava spurting out of the volcano and heard the mountain rumbling. Dad told us Arenal is over 5,500 feet tall—that's over a mile high! Wow! Now that's tall!

July 2

Oh! I can't believe our vacation will be over tomorrow. For our last adventure, we went horseback riding at my tíos' ranch. Later, we went to dinner and had one of Costa Rica's specialties, arroz con pollo. That's chicken with rice! We've had such a fantastic time with our tíos and primos, I can't wait to come back again! But the good news is that they now owe us a visit to the United States!

When I tell Clara about all the wonderful adventures I had on my vacation, I know she will wish she could have come, too! ◉

Question Cards

What were some questions you asked yourself as you read "In the Land of the Ticos"? Did you ask questions to better understand the meaning of the story or to figure out what might happen next? Did you ask questions about the author's purpose or Paula's journal entries? Write some of the questions you asked on an index card. Then trade cards with a classmate and compare your questions.

Make a Mini-Dictionary

Make a Spanish-English mini-dictionary to go along with "In the Land of the Ticos." Write down all the Spanish words from the story in alphabetical order, along with their English meanings and an illustration. If you like, add to your dictionary as you learn the meanings of other Spanish words.

Choose an Adventure

Imagine that you could join the family in the story on their vacation in Costa Rica for just one day. Which day would you choose? Why would you choose that day?

All Fired Up!

Join some of the authors of Rigby's books, stories, and articles as they share their thoughts on writing. You'll go "behind the scenes" to find out who these talented writers are and—who knows?—maybe you'll find out they're a lot like you!

Meet Our Authors

Angela Shelf Medearis

- The Wedding
- My Odd Aunt Erma Lynn

Angela Shelf Medearis lives in Texas with her husband, Michael, who is sometimes her writing partner. Angela tutors elementary school students and hosts a television book review program in addition to being a full-time writer. She says she loves being a writer because "it has given me the opportunity to travel to many different parts of the world, to meet thousands of interesting people, and to create stories I love." Besides that, she says, "I can go to work in my pajamas!"

Tim Arnold

- The Strange Case of the Bully's Lunch
- Scraping the Sky

Tim Arnold, who has worked as a teacher and illustrator, says he has always loved reading, writing, and drawing. "I read a lot when I was young," he says, "and I still do." As a child, Tim says he especially loved science fiction, and devoured "any science fiction paperbacks I could filch from my older sister's bookcase." Tim now lives in Boston, where his two children are a major part of his life. When he isn't writing or drawing, Tim likes to listen to music, read about ecology, and paint.

Mike Graf

- Special Effects, Specially Done
- The Trap
- Grandfathers Remember
- Danger Lurks Underground
- Islands of Freedom
- Fossil River Adventure

Mike Graf, who lives in Chico, California, says, "I have always been a writer. I didn't know I was going to write for a living until publishers started accepting my manuscripts!" Before he became a professional writer, Mike taught fourth and fifth grade and worked as a television weatherman. But these days, Mike is writing about the weather and the outdoors instead. He says, "I love writing about the outdoors. Whether it's weather, scenery, or outdoor action, I like to watch what is going on in our environment and write about it!" Mike hopes that his experiences looking for dinosaur bones and exploring deep, dark caves will inspire his readers to try some new adventures of their own.

Diane Bair and Pamela Wright

- A Walk in the Woods
- Wildlife Watching
- Beyond the Ordinary Camera
- Adventure Vacations
- That's Determination!

Diane Bair and Pamela Wright do their writing in a 200-year-old building near the ocean in Newburyport, Massachusetts. Their love of wildlife and the outdoors has taken this pair to a bear camp in Alaska, to gray whale breeding grounds in Mexico, and to the murky waters of Florida to snorkel with one-ton manatees. When they're not lurking behind animal blinds or tracking wolves for one of their books or magazine articles, Diane and Pam like to bike, hike, kayak, and ski. "We're usually willing to try almost anything," says Pam, and Diane agrees. "Anything that takes us outdoors!"

Tamim Ansary

- Buffalo Dreamer
- Searching for Space Rocks
- The Code Talkers
- White Streak

Tamim Ansary was born in Afghanistan, where the tradition of oral storytelling is an art. Tamim remembers listening spellbound to the stories his elders told. "My grandmother was one of the best storytellers. Some of her stories extended over three or four nights!" When he was sixteen, Tamim came to the United States to attend school. He currently lives in San Francisco with his wife, a former circus clown, and their two daughters. Tamim continues to write about topics that "connect to his own passions" and to "write from the heart as well as the brain." He also continues to tell stories to his own children in the tradition of his elders.

Katacha Díaz

- Reynaldo's Magic Stripes
- Hooked on Worms
- Home-Alone Kids

Katacha Díaz was born in Washington, D.C., but grew up in Peru, South America, where she dreamed of someday becoming an author. While growing up, she loved to tell stories and write to her many pen pals in the United States and Canada. Katacha currently lives in California, but has traveled all over the world to gather material for her stories and articles. Katacha says, "I undertake a project because I want to immerse myself in the subject and learn more about it. It's funny about favorite stories, because the story that I'm most *fired up* about is always the one that I'm working on at that particular time."

Maureen Mecozzi

- That Sinking Feeling
- Real Monsters or Myths?
- Midnight Journeys: Travels in the Mysterious World of Sleep

Maureen Mecozzi has traveled a long way from Illinois, where she grew up. She now lives in the South Asian country of Singapore, but through the Internet, Maureen says she can "stay in touch with people and events just as if I were right there in America." Maureen was a newspaper reporter and a disc jockey before she became a writer. Because she loves reading—"everything from novels to cereal boxes!"—Maureen hopes her articles and books will help students discover their own passion for reading.

Brad Herzog

- A Town Named Sue
- Buried Sunshine
- Shake, Rattle, and Roll
- Hank and Gretchen

Brad Herzog knew he wanted to be a writer when he read J. R. R. Tolkien's *The Hobbit* in the sixth grade. "It made me realize what a writer can do with his or her imagination," he says. "You can open new worlds for readers and take them on a great adventure." And that is just what Brad is doing these days. Recently, he and his wife traveled around the U.S. in a motor home to collect information for a book he was writing. When he's not on the road, Brad spends his time as a freelance writer for several magazines, including *Sports Illustrated for Kids, Reader's Digest,* and *Basketball Digest.* Brad lives with his wife and son in Pacific Grove, California.

Rigby Question-and-Answer Time

Rigby: When did you start writing?

Mike: Ever since I can remember, I've been writing stories and saving them. One of my earliest, "Tale of a Tail," was about a boy and a lion who create tornadoes without knowing it. I wrote it in the sixth grade.

Brad: I had some very special teachers who helped me become a writer. My fourth grade teacher showed me how fun it can be to be creative. My sixth grade teacher taught me the joys of reading. And I had an English teacher in high school who believed in my writing and gave me the confidence to keep doing it.

Angela: I started writing ten years ago, after I got fired from my job as a secretary. I'm a firm believer that everything works out for the best! It took four years and at least a hundred rejection letters before I got my first book published.

Tamim: The first place I turned was to the stories my elders told. Oral storytelling is a highly developed art in Afghanistan. Once I learned to read English, I had another huge pool of stories to tap into, and I had my nose in a book pretty much all the time. Then I started writing stories.

Maureen: I started my writing career as editor of a newsletter we published in sixth grade. It had a lot of silly jokes and some cartoons. But even the principal had a subscription!

Katacha: When I was a little girl growing up in Peru, I dreamed of being a writer. I loved to tell stories. I wrote my first story in a letter to my grandparents, who were living in France.

Rigby: You began writing at such a young age, Katacha! By now it must seem almost effortless to you.

Katacha: I don't think that writing is ever effortless. Sometimes the characters just pop onto the computer screen and the story seems almost to write itself. Other times, coming up with a new idea is a bit of a struggle. During these times, I take my dog for a walk or ride my bicycle into the country. It helps me tremendously!

Rigby: What do you like to write about? What gets you really *fired up*?

Mike: I love writing about the outdoors. When I am traveling to great places like our national parks, I get inspired to write, and great story ideas come to me.

Tim: I try to remember things from my own childhood that seem true, then write about them.

Brad: I like to write about people, places, and things that deserve to be written about. I also like to write funny stories. It makes me happy to know that someone reading one of my stories might laugh out loud.

Diane and Pam: We enjoy writing about adventure travel and outdoor fun. We like to put readers right in the middle of the action—like on a giant film screen, only with words.

Rigby: Diane and Pam, you always write as a team. How does that work for you?

Diane and Pam: In researching our book, *Wild Encounters,* we traveled across the country in search of exciting places to watch animals. We enjoyed sharing that with our readers. Our job is fun! Of course, being a travel writer means you have to read a lot about the places you visit. And you have to love to write. We do!

Rigby: What would you most like to say to kids through your writing?

Diane and Pam: We would like to tell kids to learn about the world around you; respect and protect nature; go out there, be aware, and have fun!

Katacha: My ultimate goal is to amuse, inspire, and educate my readers, so that they, too, can go on an adventure. Who knows? Maybe some of my readers will become writers, too!

Maureen: When you read, you can explore new places and ideas and meet amazing people on every page. I hope my words do that for Rigby readers.

Do any of these authors' experiences sound like yours? How can you find out more about these authors?

Stop and Respond

Ask Anything

Choose any author, either living now or long ago, that you would really like to talk to. Then think of three questions you would ask that person about the content, meaning, and style of his or her work.

Book Talk

Select three books by the same author or three books on a similar subject or theme. Give an informal book talk to your class in which you do your best to convince everyone to read these books. Be prepared to answer questions about the books you've read.

Authors' Tips

Based on what you learned in "All Fired Up!" and what you already know about the lives and work of different authors, think about the personal qualities people need to succeed as authors. Discuss your ideas with a partner, and then work together to make a list of tips for people who want to be authors.

Behind the Picture

Select an interesting photograph from a magazine and use it to write a story. Your story, which can be serious or funny, should focus on what happened just before the picture was taken.

The Show Goes On!

Have you ever noticed jobs such as "gaffer" and "best boy" in movie credits and wondered what those jobs were? Find out about all the "behind-the-scene" jobs that need to be done to make a movie. Then write a glossary of movie jobs. List the different jobs in alphabetical order and describe them.

Eureka!

Suppose that you could interview a famous scientist or inventor. What would you ask that person about his or her discovery or invention? Write a dialogue between you and the inventor. Then, with a partner role play the parts of the famous person and the interviewer. After you and your partner practice reading the dialogue aloud, perform your skit for an audience.

When I was young, I was always...

What made you want to become a scientist?

More Books

Finch, Christopher, Charles S. Finch and Jim Henson. *The Works: The Art, the Magic, the Imagination*. Random House, 1993.

Kovacs, Deborah and James Preller. *Meet the Authors and Illustrators: Volume 1*. Scholastic Trade, 1999.

Hahn, Don. *Animation Magic: A Behind-the-Scenes Look at How an Animated Film Is Made*. Disney, 2000.

Lasky, Kathryn. *The Most Beautiful Roof in the World*. Harcourt, 1997.

Scott, Elaine. *Movie Magic: Behind the Scenes with Special Effects*. Morrow, 1995.

Denny, Roz. *A Taste of India*. Thomson Learning, 1997.

On the Web

Rain Forests
http://passporttoknowledge.com/
　　rainforest/main.html
http://www.cloudforestalive.org

Special Effects
http://visualmagic.awn.com

India
http://www.bawarchi.com/festivals/
　　sankranti.html

Across the Curriculum

Art
Choose a play you've seen or one that your class has read or performed. Design sets or costumes for the play. Draw some of your ideas.

Social Studies
Investigate a holiday, celebration, or festival from another country. Describe the reason for the event, the customs associated with it, and how the participants prepare for it.

patent pending

A Blast from the Past

Writers have always wondered about all sorts of things. Get a blast from the past as you read the wonderings and wisdom of these great writers who lived fifty, one hundred—even two hundred years ago!

On dreams and following them

Hitch your wagon to a star.

Ralph Waldo Emerson

All that we see or seem is but a dream within a dream.

Edgar Allan Poe

On friendship

Piglet sidled up to Pooh from behind. "Pooh!" he whispered. "Yes, Piglet?" "Nothing," said Piglet, taking Pooh's paw. "I just wanted to be sure of you."

A. A. Milne

On happiness and kindness

There might be some credit in being jolly.

Charles Dickens

Think of all the beauty still around you and be happy.

Anne Frank

Just for fun

I ask only to be free. The butterflies are free.

Ralph Waldo Emerson

"Well, now that we have seen each other," said the Unicorn, "if you believe in me, I'll believe in you. Is that a bargain?"

Lewis Carroll

"The time has come," the Walrus said, "to talk of many things:
Of shoes—and ships—and sealing wax—
Of cabbages—and kings—
And why the sea is boiling hot—
And whether pigs have wings."

Lewis Carroll

On writing

The difference between the almost right word and the right word is really a large matter—'tis the difference between the lightning bug and the lightning.

Mark Twain

It is not often that someone comes along who is a true friend, and a good writer.

E. B. White, from Charlotte's Web